The Work of Jean Dubuffet, 1901–

by Peter Selz with texts by the artist · The Museum of Modern Art, N.Y.

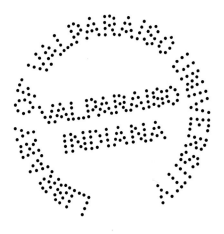

Published by the Museum of Modern Art, 1962
11 West 53 Street, New York 19, N. Y.
All rights reserved
Library of Congress Catalogue Card No. 62–11971
Designed by Susan Draper
Printed in Germany by Brüder Hartmann, West Berlin

Contents

Acknowledgments 7

Jean Dubuffet: The Earlier Work – *by Peter Selz* 9

Landscaped Tables, Landscapes of the Mind,
Stones of Philosophy – *by Jean Dubuffet* 63

Memoir on the Development of My Work
from 1952 – *by Jean Dubuffet* 73

Jean Dubuffet: The Recent Work – *by Peter Selz* 139

Statement on Paintings of 1961 – *by Jean Dubuffet* 165

Notes to the Text 166

Major Exhibitions 169

Bibliography 171

Index to Illustrations 185

FOR FRANCES PERNAS

Acknowledgments

This book is being published on the occasion of The Museum of Modern Art's retrospective exhibition of the work of Jean Dubuffet which will be shown also at The Art Institute of Chicago and the Los Angeles County Museum of Art. On behalf of the Trustees of the three museums, I wish first to thank Jean Dubuffet not only for his gracious cooperation and assistance, but also for providing us with his enlightening *Memoir* as well as the jacket design for this book. Second only to the artist himself, I am obliged to Noël Arnaud, for supplying us with much of the essential documentation.

I am indebted to Mrs. Louise Varèse for her excellent translation of the *Memoir*, to Arnold Newman for his portrait of the artist which serves as the frontispiece, to Thalia Selz for her help in editing the manuscript, and Alfred H. Barr, Jr. for his suggestions. I want to thank Lucy Lippard for translations and research and Bernard Karpel and Inga Forslund for preparing the bibliography, Alicia Legg for preparing the catalogue of the exhibition, which is printed separately, and Therese Varveris for her efficient help.

Pierre Matisse has encouraged this project from its inception and has been of great assistance with information. In addition we are obliged to him for his permission to reprint the introduction to his catalogue "Landscaped Tables, Landscapes of the Mind, Stones of Philosophy." Particular thanks are also extended to Thomas M. Messer with whom I originally discussed both book and exhibition when he was Director of the Institute of Contemporary Art in Boston. I furthermore wish to acknowledge the help of François Mathey, Curator of the Musée des Arts Décoratifs in Paris, and Edouard Morot-Sir, Cultural Counselor of the French Embassy in New York.

For special assistance, I want to thank Joachim Jean Aberbach, Julian J. Aberbach, Mr. and Mrs. James W. Alsdorf, Mr. and Mrs. Gordon Bunshaft, Mr. and Mrs. Ralph F. Colin, Robert Elkon, Mr. and Mrs. Alex Hillman, Mr. and Mrs. Arnold H. Maremont, Mr. and Mrs. Morton G. Neumann, Jacques Sarlie, Mr. and Mrs. David M. Solinger, G. David Thompson, and Mr. and Mrs. Sam Zacks.

Peter Selz

Jean Dubuffet. 1961. Photo Arnold Newman

Jean Dubuffet: The Earlier Work – *by Peter Selz*

A few months after the Liberation, in October 1944, at the Galerie René Drouin in Paris, Jean Dubuffet held his first exhibition. Dubuffet was forty-three, an age at which so many artists of the youth-conscious, novelty-seeking twentieth century have already uttered their brief messages. He was at no time a "young artist." The work which he presented at this exhibition had all been done since 1942 and marked his third attempt to become a painter.

Since that time Dubuffet's output has been truly enormous. This artist, whose creative energy is prodigious, has completed over 5,000 works, including about 1,600 oils, 77 sculptures, 480 lithographs, as well as gouaches, drawings, imprints, assemblages of various kinds, woodcuts, illustrated books, etc.

Born of a middle-class family in Le Havre in 1901, he went to Paris to study painting at the Académie Julian in 1918. After six months, finding academic training distasteful, he withdrew to paint and draw in his own studio. He met Suzanne Valadon, and an early drawing of his grandmother in its simple, definite linear structure shows an interest in her draftsmanship.

But Dubuffet deliberately stayed aloof from art movements; he turned to music and began playing the piano, bagpipe and accordion. Over the years this interest has become wider, and he finds time to amuse himself and his friends by playing exotic instruments for them.

During his early youthful days in Paris, he met Max Jacob and grew interested in poetry, including Jacob's ambiguous puns and ironic statements on the commonplace, which were later to find a parallel in Dubuffet's own art. He became involved in the study of ancient and modern languages. Someone gave him Dr. Hans Prinzhorn's book, *Bildnerei der Geisteskranken*,[1] and here he first experienced the power of psychopathic art which seemed to him more intense in its brutal strength than the "art of the museums." He entered the meteorological service of the Army and was stationed at the Eiffel Tower where he could observe the city from above. (In the forties he was to examine it more closely for the purpose of revealing its backstreets, but these previous bird's-eye views also became ingrained in his memory.) He traveled to Italy in 1923 and to Brazil in 1924. Returning to Le Havre in 1925, he embarked upon his first marriage, and in 1930 he founded a small wholesale wine business in Paris. He felt that the

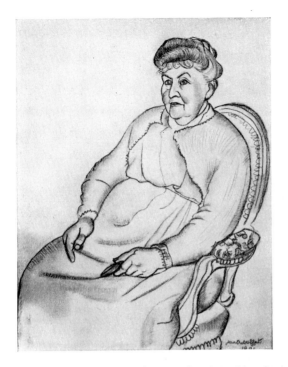

Portrait of Mme Arthur Dubuffet, Grand-mother of the Artist. 1921. Pencil and sanguine, 18⅛ × 14⅛". Owned by the artist

simple, everyday life of the common people contained more art and poetry than did academic study or "great painting." The latter he found isolated from life, pretentious and boring. In 1946, when he wrote the revealing *Prospectus aux amateurs de tout genre*, he explained that he aims not "at the mere gratification of a handful of specialists, but would much rather amuse and interest the man in the street when he comes home from work. ... It is the man in the street that I'm after, whom I feel closest to, with whom I want to make friends and enter into confidence and connivance, and *he* is the one I want to please and enchant by means of my work ..."[2]

It may be argued that his image of irony and paradox is not the sort of thing which becomes a truly popular image. Dubuffet, after all, is a discoverer not an entertainer. The masses, feeling the need of identification, naturally prefer Brigitte Bardot to a Dubuffet Corps de Dame.

If the official world of art was of no interest to Dubuffet, neither could the wine business satisfy him for long. Giving it up in 1934, he began to search for a popular art form, in which everyone could take part and by which everyone could be entertained. Soon his house on rue Lhomond, where he moved in 1935 with Emilie Carlu—his second wife "Lili"—became a workshop, a theater, a little carnival. There he played the accordion for his friends and made life-masks of their faces. Working in plaster, he became for the first time decisively involved with tactile material as the plaster changed, grew hot, solidified and seemed to have an organic life of its own. He started a puppet show and carved wooden marionettes, again using his friends for models. Soon thereafter, he began to paint again quite spontaneously. These were mostly pictures of Lili, rather naïve in conception as well as execution. His masks, puppets and paintings met with no success whatsoever and, doubting his own talents, he finally gave up his activity as an artist and returned to the wine business in 1937, a career which was interrupted briefly in 1939 by his conscription into the army. Due to his lack of discipline, he was stationed at the garrison of Rochefort and then quickly demobilized.

By 1942 he was again occupied with painting. But, having looked at the art of the Western tradition in a great many museums and being surrounded by art in Paris, he first had to decerebrate himself—strip himself of acquired culture—in order to be able to locate an earlier state of childlike innocence and amazement. Klee, whom he admires, had taken a similar road into the elementary and formative beginnings of art, and Dubuffet is the only French artist who has a full understanding of the work of Paul Klee.

He painted the fields and houses in the green countryside outside Paris, sometimes animated by little figures, in a strange up-tilted perspective. His subjects were awkward cows and ener-

Papier mâché masks. 1935. Left to right: Robert Polguère, André Claude, René Pontier. Collection Mme Henri-Pierre Roché, Bellevue, s/o, France

getic milkmaids or nude and monstrous lady bicyclists riding their odd contraptions straight at the spectator. He rendered intimate observations of city life. In the beginning these pictures were brilliantly colored, recalling the palette of the Fauves, or rather the Brücke painters, with their startling juxtaposition of large discordant color patches. Indeed, his response to the city, as seen in the early Views of Paris and the Métro pictures, has unexpected resemblances to Kirchner's street scenes, done in Dresden and Berlin before World War I—not only in their color, but even more significantly, in the psychological impact produced by thrusting the individual into a cramped space crowded with people with whom no relationship can be established.

Dubuffet chose to paint the Parisians on their daily journey in the Métro. Here they are, more like cattle in their stalls than human beings, their funny hats an integral part of their faces. Heads and bodies are drawn crudely, as though by a child, according to the simplest schemes of frontal and profile view. From the very beginning, Dubuffet dismisses perspective

Woman on a Bicycle. 1944. Gouache, $12^5/8 \times 9^7/8''$. Collection André Berne-Joffroy, Paris

opposite: *Blissful Countryside.* 1944. Oil on canvas, $50 \times 34''$. Collection Mrs. Maurice E. Culberg, Chicago

13

in favor of a more innocent and direct presentation of space. And here in the Métro the use of two-dimensional space, with depth indicated solely by the crude method of overlapping, yields the cramped effect most graphically. The artist looks with fresh amazement at human behavior, at these stylized figures staring vapidly into space, rigidly standing and seated as if they were performing some strange ritual (page 16).

Much more intimate, yet conversely even more hieratic, is *Childbirth* of March 1944. This painting "captures the naïveté of votive pictures; it is like those thank offerings found in pilgrimage churches and presents a comparable aspect of ritual, of 'emotion recollected in tranquility.'"[3]

His views of the streets of Paris have a similar familiarity with the subject, a comparable intimacy. He shuns the grand boulevards where Monet and Pissarro perceived their people as though they were sparkling symptoms of a diffuse atmosphere. He goes to the narrow back-streets and paints the old façades of high tenements, peopled with de-personalized stick figures leaning out of their windows for a breath of air or standing aimlessly in the streets. He paints these narrow streets and alleys with their pathetic little wine and coal shops and bars. These are the streets where the riders of Dubuffet's Métro go to live and eat and sleep. The artist has depicted this disparaged world with the mixture of cruelty and tenderness which is peculiar to his humor (page 17).

Then, from the façades, he went on to look more closely at the pavements and the walls themselves. His "Messages" (page 20) are derived from the inscriptions on old, crumbling walls: the graffiti which have become so popular since Dubuffet and Brassai called attention to them. Giacomo Balla had previously depicted the silent poignancy of wall scribblings in his prophetic *Bankrupt* of 1902, and Max Ernst anticipated some of Dubuffet's themes and techniques in his *Histoire naturelle* of 1925. But where Balla communicated an aspect of human tragedy and pathos, and Ernst's *frottages* have an obsessive dream-like quality, Dubuffet's Messages are much more matter-of-fact in their statement. For Ernst (as for Leonardo da Vinci[4]) the painter's associations and discoveries were decisive; Dubuffet, like the great photographer Brassai,[5] relies on the associations evoked in the mind and eye of the viewer.

Mixing gouaches and inks and working on old newspapers, he reproduced these ephemeral communications on man's loneliness, needs and desires. Then he turned to the decaying walls

Childbirth. 1944. Oil on canvas, 39³/₈ × 31³/₄″. Private collection

Métro. 1943. Oil on canvas, 63³/₄ × 51¹/₈″. Private collection

View of Paris — The Life of Pleasure. 1944. Oil on canvas, $35 \times 45^{3}/_{4}''$. Collection Mr. and Mrs. David M. Solinger, New York

Grand nu charbonneux. 1944. Oil on canvas, 13³/₄ × 38¹/₄". Collection
Carlo Frua de Angeli, Milan

themselves; beguiled by the old and venerable stone, he revealed a new beauty which his selective eye discovered, he transmuted the surfaces and textures of the walls to new lithographic stone and made a suite of thirteen lithographs, illustrating Guillevic's poems *Les Murs*, documenting the dilapidated surfaces with their cracks, holes and scribbles. Or, he drew with coal as a child might. Indeed, the rejection of any form of central composition in favor of a continuous fragment, as well as the close examination of the texture of substance and material, remain constant concerns in Dubuffet's work, indicating his affinity to naïve conception.

Once he began observing the material—the stone, cement itself—color, in the sense of pigment, became a matter quite foreign to his world. One day in August of 1944 in the Jardin des Plantes, he was less impressed with the flowers than with the blocks of anthracite, basalt, graphite that he saw. This dark, monochromatic material has a life and vitality of its own. Thus inspired, he painted his first large nude, the *Grand nu charbonneux*. This extraordinary painting not only holds all the premonitions of the Corps de Dames, but with its clumsy, awkward stance, its gesture of exclamatory display, its cruel but loving outline, its naïve emphasis on sex, it is one of the strongest and boldest nudes in modern painting.

His walls take on an extraordinary beauty of texture as in *The Smoker by a Wall*, or is it the artist's rich textures which resemble a wall? This dapper young man-about-town sports a modish hat, dangles a cigarette and enjoys the special distinction of the large red square of paint which he wears in the middle of his cheek the way a more respectable personage would wear his beribboned medal (page 21).

In his efforts to find the popular imagery which would amuse and enchant rather than elevate, he turned to jazz for his subject matter. In December 1944, Dubuffet, an admirer of Duke Ellington, completed three large canvases of jazz musicians, their combos lined up across the picture plane in a static frieze. The isocephalism and the repetitive grimaces stamping each face offer the spectator a naïve account of jazz musicians as they might appear to the bemused observer (page 23).

His subjects are common people and most ordinary occurrences; his form is rather closely related to wall scratchings and to children's art. Soon he will also turn to the use of coarse and unrefined materials. His proclamation that "my art is an attempt to bring all disparaged values into the limelight"[6] is a key to the interpretation of all his work. It accounts for his subjects—the

19

walls of old buildings, jazz musicians, drilling dentists, old tables and stones, Bowery bums. It clarifies his opposition to classical beauty and his interest in the values of barbarism, in the art of the simple-minded, the untrained, the psychopaths; it explains his various techniques, his use of the bark and leaves of trees, of tar, asphalt and putty, and of clinkers and old sponges in his sculpture.

In May 1946, his second major exhibition, entitled *Mirobolus Macadam & Cie / Hautes Pâtes*, opened at the Galerie Drouin, causing a scandal. These forty-eight paintings alarmed the public by their imagery of cruel irony (few people realized how funny they were) and by their use of crude materials. In the best dada tradition, paintings were slashed by infuriated spectators. Many of the critics were wildly antagonistic and, in fact, nothing had so outraged the Paris art world in a great many years. It must be borne in mind that at that time the most "advanced" work to be seen in Paris was at the annual salons of the Réalités Nouvelles which included multitudes of anemic geometric abstractions in which the paint was applied with a thin and impersonal uniformity. Now this! Critics accused Dubuffet quite correctly of anarchy;

Merci beaucoup ma santé toujours excellente . . . . 1944.
Gouache and ink, 8⁷/₈×10¹/₂″. Private collection

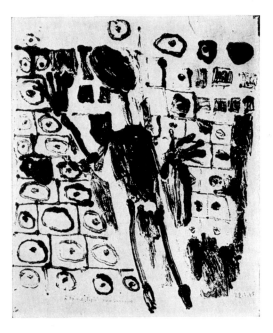

Man in Front of a Wall. 1945. Printer's ink,
13³/₈×11³/₈″. Collection D. B. C.

The Smoker by a Wall. 1945. Oil on canvas, $45^{7}/_{8} \times 31^{7}/_{8}''$. Collection Julian and Joachim Jean Aberbach, New York

less accurate was their talk of "ephemeral success." They were revolted by his use of mud, his "scrapings of the dust bin." Words like *merde* and *cacaïsme* made their appearance. Several critics were perceptive enough to recognize a similarity to Jarry and *Ubu Roi*, and it is certainly true that Jarry provided an important source for Dubuffet's imagery. The comparison, however, was usually made perjoratively by the critics, like René Huyghe,[7] but, in spite of all this opposition, the 1946 show was sold out within days.[8]

In his Hautes Pâtes—Thick Impastoes—Dubuffet no longer finds it possible to apply oil paint with a brush. Antagonistic to the acceptance of traditional craftsmanship, having been impressed by the study of the walls and all the implications of walls and graffiti, he now develops a paste in which he can slash, scratch and dig; where he can physically, manually, go beneath the surface. He prepares a hard and resistant substance made up of asphalt, tar and white lead, enriching the basic paste with cement, plaster, varnishes and glues as well as lime, sand, coal dust, pebbles, pieces of glass, string, straw, etc. Indeed, he has scraped the junk pile as well as the dust bin.

Like the dadaists, Dubuffet loves materials, especially old and discarded materials, but whereas the dadaists and their followers cherish the use of heterogeneous materials for their own sake, Dubuffet combines them into a new and denser unity, a new substance which becomes his essential reality. He, moreover, shares with dada and surrealism his dependence on chance, his interest in automatism, although he always retains a controlling hand. His desire to shock stodgy bourgeois society, his anti-art attitude, his "anticultural position" differ from the previous challenges in expressionism, futurism, dada and surrealism in his individual stance, in his refusal to participate in group agitations. He may have innumerable followers, but he is part of no school or movement.

Dubuffet applies his thick impasto mixture to various supports: masonite, composition board, canvas. Before the paste is allowed to harden, he traces lines with a spoon, knife, a trowel, or his fingers, the way people write their initials or draw hearts in wet cement. We are reminded of the signatures of movie stars scratched into the pavement of Grauman's Chinese Theater under the flashbulbs of Hollywood.

The material with which, or rather *in* which he works, is of the greatest importance now. This is no longer a mere means to an end; it has become essential, speaks its own language,

opposite: *Grand Jazz Band (New Orleans)*. 1944. Oil on canvas, 45$^{1}/_{8}$ × 57$^{5}/_{8}$". Collection Mr. and Mrs. Gordon Bunshaft, New York

Minerva. 1945. Oil and various materials on canvas, 36$^1/_4$ × 25$^5/_8$". Private collection, Turin

Touring Club. 1946. Oil and various materials on canvas, 38¹/₄ × 51¹/₄". Collection Richard S. Zeisler, New York

Leader in a Parade Uniform. 1945. Oil and various materials on canvas, $36^{1}/_{4} \times 25^{1}/_{2}"$. Collection Mr. and Mrs. Morton G. Neumann, Chicago

The Coffee Grinder. 1945. Oil and various materials on canvas, 45½×35″. Collection Mr. and Mrs. Ralph F. Colin, New York

Limbour, Chicken Droppings. 1946. Oil emulsion on composition board, $43^{1}/_{4} \times 30^{3}/_{4}$". Private collection

Lili in Metallic Black. 1946. Oil on masonite, $42^7/_8 \times 34^5/_8$". Collection Mr. and Mrs. Irving Richards, New York

helps determine the result. Dubuffet's actual performance is rather close to the principles of Henri Focillon who urges us to "abandon the isolated consideration of form, matter, tool and hand," and speaks of a new "quadruple alliance" which he calls "the touch" that "represents a single moment, in which the tool awakens form in the substance."[9]

The element of chance is welcomed, although channeled toward the artist's final aim. Dubuffet is the prestidigitator who uses the accident to perform his sorcery. The articulation resulting in the end is the product of the play among the artist's hand, his mental image and the nature of the material. Important as the material is to him, he never permits it to gain the upper hand; his attitude is never one of passive acceptance, but neither does he merely execute a preconceived image. He speaks of a dialogue between the artist and his materials and tools. The working process for him is a matter of adventure and discovery.

The light in the Hautes Pâtes is the light that emerges slowly in a dark room and persists more enduringly once it is discerned. The color is largely limited to that inherent in the material itself; it is a factor of the substance used. The objects are flattened out two-dimensionally on the rectangular surface, pushing the image immediately forward to be seen and experienced at close range. In his *Touring Club* (page 25), the four riders cram the car, which, in turn, is swollen to fill the picture plane. These passengers are reminiscent of the cramped carriage ride to the funeral in Joyce's *Ulysses*, with its impinging of objects on flesh, flesh on flesh, ideas on fragmentary associations and, above all, of words on the reader. As in *Ulysses*, we are strikingly aware of the material itself.

These figures of 1945 to 1947 are shocking only if approached with preconceived notions of classical "beauty." Ugliness and beauty do not exist for Dubuffet as he becomes fascinated with the relation of nature (his material) to man (the emerging image). He loves to make much of the wrinkles, deformations, grimaces of the sitter, but he is by no means concerned with the individuality of the person. In fact, he purposely de-personalizes and is more interested in the common features shared by all men, finding sanction for this in the effigies of Egyptian sarcophagi, "Chinese imperial figures," medieval coins.[10]

The "Macadam" series anticipated in certain ways the great series of portraits (pages 28, 29, 32, 33, 35). His aim in portraiture is the prevention of easy recognition by his emphasis on specific fortuitous details—a hairy ear, long teeth, etc.—in order to stimulate the imagination of the spectator and augment the power of the image. Completely ignoring the prevalent opinion of contemporary painters and critics that the portrait is *passé*, Dubuffet painted these "likenesses" of his friends. But he rightly condemns the misinterpretation of his portraits as having "psychological insight." One assumes that these are penetrating images of the human psyche because they so often astonish us with wild, uncanny, obscene or hilarious suggestions of our own states of mind as represented in our appearances. Dubuffet, however, has simply abstracted certain expressions and physiognomical characteristics found commonly enough in the human race and employed them to display his own vivid sense of irony and amazement when confronted by the human comedy. We compliment him on psychological understanding when we should salute him for those qualities far more important for a painter: a ferociously keen eye and extraordinarily fecund invention.

Certain accessories constantly recur, at least on the clothed figures: the hat which is part of the face, the buttons which assume the importance they have in children's drawings, the necktie and large watch as signs of bourgeois respectability. The female figure is equipped with certain obvious symbols: many of them wear large round medals with male profiles around their necks and centered above the circles of their breasts. The *Cafetière* of 1945 has a coffee grinder between her legs.

"People are more handsome than they think they are. Long live their true faces at the Galerie René Drouin, 17, Place Vendôme. Portraits with a resemblance extracted, with resemblance cooked and conserved in the memory, with a resemblance exploded in the memory of Mr. Jean Dubuffet, painter"[11]—was the announcement on the little folding catalogue designed like a newspaper by Dubuffet himself for his exhibition of portraits in October 1947 (37 paintings and 35 drawings).

The above legend was followed in the catalogue by a "Causette," a little chat by the artist which begins: "What interests me is not cake but bread . . ."[11]

Yet for his sitters, he uses many of the leading poets and writers of his generation who are his friends and many of whom had already served as models for his life masks some ten years earlier. They include the critic and spokesman for *art autre* and *art informel*, Michel Tapié; the poet, novelist and critic, Georges Limbour—Dubuffet's school companion in Le Havre who was a member of the surrealist movement from its beginnings, as well as the first important writer

Fautrier with Wrinkled Brow. 1947. Oil on canvas, $45^5/8 \times 35''$. Robert Elkon Gallery, New York

Joë Bousquet in Bed. 1947. Oil on canvas, 57⅝ × 44⅞″. The Museum of Modern Art, New York. Mrs. Simon Guggenheim Fund

on Dubuffet. There are several portraits of his wife Lili and of his dealers, René Drouin and Pierre Matisse.[12] He portrays the painters, Jean Fautrier and Gaston Chaissac and the draftsman and poet, Henri Michaux. There are poignantly descriptive portraits of the poet Joë Bousquet who, paralyzed in World War I, lived for thirty-three years in the obscure town of Narbonne near Carcasonne, writing dream-infused verse, essays and reminiscences of a delicate yet piercing power. There are the writer, Francis Ponge, erstwhile intellectual leader of the Resistance Movement, who is akin to Dubuffet in the minute analyses of animal, vegetable and mineral life; Jean Paulhan (Maast), the famous essayist and critic who for twenty years was editor of the *Nouvelle Revue Française*; Antonin Artaud, poet and actor who overshot surreal-

Dentist. 1947. Colored inks, $14^{1}/_{2} \times 12^{5}/_{8}$". Collection Dr. Ch. Hulin, Peyzac Le Moustier, Dordogne, France

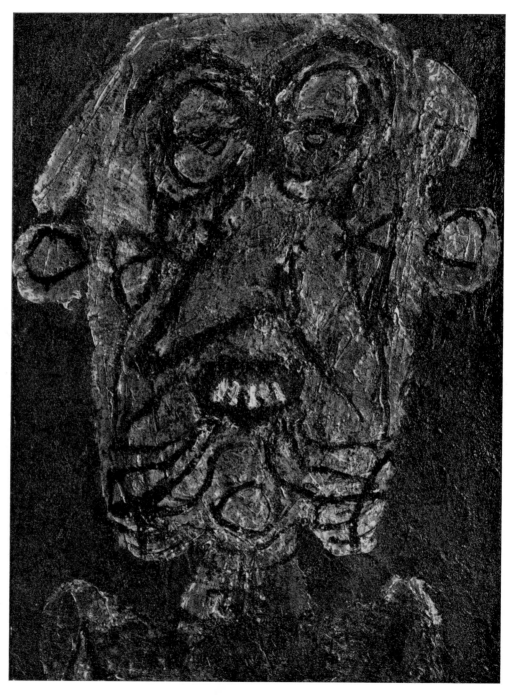

Jules Supervielle, Large Banner Portrait. 1947. Oil on canvas, $51^{1}/_{2} \times 38^{1}/_{2}''$. The Art Institute of Chicago. Gift of Mr. and Mrs. Maurice E. Culberg

Arab and Palm Trees. 1947–48. Distemper, 17³/₄ × 21⁵/₈". Private collection

Arab and Palm Tree. 1947–48. Gouache, 17¹/₂ × 22". Collection Edward Dragon, East Hampton, New York

ist theory to such a degree that he appeared insane; Paul Léautaud, writer, anthologist, critic and editor of the *Mercure de France*; André Dhotel, whose novels of the forties and fifties mark a survival of surrealism; the novelists Pierre Benoit (now a member of the French Academy) and Marcel Jouhandeau (pseudonym for Marcel Provence), the fantasist poet and playwright, Jules Supervielle; the poetess, Edith Boissonnas; and the poet and critic, René Bertelé.

These faces which look so absurd seem to liberate the individual from his own likeness. They, like the Hautes Pâtes, are de-personalized. This is perhaps another example of the swing away from emphasis on the individual and toward merging with a group which is characteristic of contemporary society. Dubuffet gives us Women Types and Men Types, broken down into such categories as Funny Women, Threatening Women, Whore Women, Weak Men, Scared Men, Appalled Men, Demonic Men, etc. Of course, the ironic aspect of his work is so strong that these individuals resemble caricatures, and one ends up with a whole gallery of startling aspects of the old universal types that might belong to a new kind of epic—the "ironic epic." Like Beckett, Ionesco and Genet, Dubuffet finds that only a ritual sort of comedy can adequately deal with the human condition.

The series of portraits was interrupted in January 1947 by a small group of drawings and gouaches of dentists (page 34), in which his irony is carried to an extreme: we identify with the patient sitting anxiously in his chair, his open mouth full of hard teeth and instruments, submitting to the tormentor's fastidious power.[13] ("Art," he says, "should always make us laugh a little and frighten us a little, but never bore us."[14]

Included in the Portrait exhibition in October 1947 were six pictures of the Sahara. He went there for the first time in March of that year to return in November for a six-months' stay and again in March 1949. A French painter traveling to North Africa sounds quite traditional. He had, after all, been preceded by Delacroix, Chassériau, Fromentin, Gérome and Matisse.

More truly romantic than his predecessors, he did not look at Africa through the condescending eyes of a member of higher civilization who would bring back picturesque paintings of the exotic life across the seas. His African pictures resemble Delacroix' canvases of sensuous yet measured vitality as little as they do Fromentin's stilted renditions of the life of colorful natives, or Gérome's titillating scenes of bazaars and slave markets. Nor did Dubuffet cross the Mediterannean to discover "faraway" colors and simplified shapes and come back from Kairouan with sensitive transparent watercolors of fairy-tale enchantment as Klee and Macke had done in 1914.

Dubuffet went far into the desert, having learned Arabic in order to communicate with the people living in the isolation of the oases of El Goléa, Hoggar, Béni-Abbés. He made capricious gouaches of the life he observed: mustachioed and bearded nomads in burnoose and turban, riding on camels or standing next to palm trees, Bedouins astride donkeys, flute players and story tellers, and Arabs wearing colorful shawls and scarves or firing guns. Fascinated by traces in material, he made drawings of the imprint of human tracks in the sand.

Back in Paris, he did a small number of larger paintings in oil and mixed media on the Sahara theme, depicting amusing figures of Arabs in profile or full face. Returning to the austere and barren sandscape of the Sahara once more, he began painting, not the transparent quality of the light, but the apparently opaque solidity of the sand. Rather than the fluid mobility of the dunes, the permanence of the desert was his concern. He painted gouaches which leave almost no room for the vast desert skies, and, characteristically, his horizon line is high as he fills his space with sand.

Arab on a Camel. 1947–48. Gouache, 12¼×16¼". Private collection

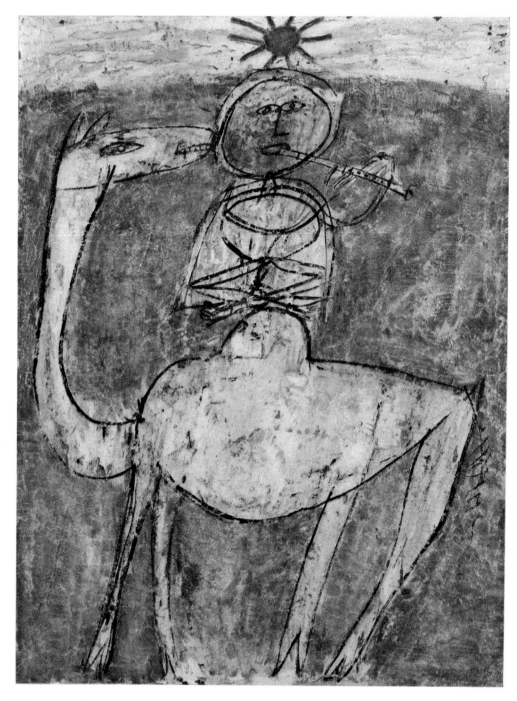

Fluting on the Hump. 1947. Oil on masonite, 46^1/$_2$ × 35^1/$_2$". Private collection, New York

Landscape with Drunkards. 1949. Oil on burlap, 35 × 45$^{1}/_{2}$". Private collection

The Man with a Rose. 1949. Distemper on canvas, 45^1/2 × 34″. Collection Mrs. Maurice
E. Culberg, Chicago

Dubuffet is indeed more thoroughly romantic than his forerunners. His complete rejection of classical values for "barbarism" and his emphasis on the irrational go much further than theirs. In the desert pictures we find him beginning to weld together animal, person and landscape into an ambiguous, mystic whole. This aspect of feeling at one with the universe was carried on in the Grotesque Landscapes (Paysages Grotesques) of 1949 and especially in the landscapes, Texturologies, Topographies, and Phenomena of later years.

The landscape now remained a permanent subject for Dubuffet, but this is always polarized with his interest in the human image. In May 1949 he painted *The Man with a Rose*, a tender and disarming comment on human emotion, a subtle and lyrical statement about the awkwardness of gallantry, done in soft powdery distemper (page 41).

Between May 1949 and January 1950, he painted a series of grotesquely animated landscapes; here he traced his line into a fairly thin, light-colored paste which he applied over a darker ground, so that the scratched line becomes dark within its white surroundings. The landscapes have an arbitrary freedom of execution which lends them a childlike freshness and charm. The generally light color conveys a feeling of spring. He jam-packs his surfaces with lines and scratches, abrasions and tracks to indicate roads, paths, houses, people, trees, animals and unidentified topographical features. Everything in these crowded little worlds impinges upon the other objects without establishing a unified or organized relationship. A dark painting like the disjunctive *Man in the Country* of 1949 might well be called a visual representation of the stream of conciousness. And, indeed, it seems to be painted almost automatically with a minimum of control resulting in complete pell-mell. "The artist must be harnessed to chance," he writes, "it's not a dance to be danced alone, but by two; chance is one of us. It pulls in both directions, while the artist steers as well as he can, but with flexibility, applies himself to making the best of every accident as it occurs, forcing it to serve his ends . . ."[15] (page 45).

The dissociation in many of the Grotesque Landscapes is due to certain objects being shown in side-elevation, others from the front, above, below. The final effect produced by these differing perspectives is indeed grotesque—an ironically apt conception of a contemporary scene which is crowded, busy and noisy but seldom intimate. Of particular interest as a transitional work, is the small *Desert Track* of July 1949 (page 44), showing little stick-figure men who "hang on" to a road like bats clinging to beams. While based on his memories of the

Sahara, its expanse of encrusted earth filling the total space in all directions as well as its execution of thick emulsion prefigures his later Soils and Terrains (Sols et Terrains).

The Paysages Grotesques in general are an outgrowth of Dubuffet's pursuit of the automatic and the uncontrolled which has engaged him for a long time. His predilection for the spontaneous as well as the barbaric, his complete rejection of objective standards, his romantic interest in the untrained "folk," and his stress on unbridled invention, imagination and fantasy led to his occupation with *l'art brut*.

He was always fascinated by the strange world on the frontier of reason. Convinced that ideas and intellectuals are enemies of art,[16] he began a systematic search for "true art," untouched by artistic culture and unspoiled by contact with the Western classic tradition. Dubuffet has little use for the professional artist whom he compares to the professional sweetheart. He acclaims, instead, the spontaneity of the amateur. He takes much stock in the visions of clairvoyants and the objects created by them. These may be the results of visions, presentiments and apparitions, or they may be effigies of exorcism and much more powerful than the rarified works of the civilized elite. He believes that there is no separate psychotic art but that the mechanism of creation among the insane is exactly the same as that among so-called normal artists, indeed, that the distinction between "normal" and "abnormal" is untenable. The creative act, accompanied by its feverish tension and frenzy, goes beyond everyday existence and "madness lightens man and gives him wings and helps him to attain visions."[17]

Dubuffet's interest in psychotic art goes back to his first reading of Prinzhorn's book when he was a youth. Later he traveled to Heidelberg to see the drawings and sculptures of the insane collected by Dr. Prinzhorn. Georges Limbour tells us[18] that he had his first contact with a clairvoyant during his army service in 1923 and that shortly thereafter he began correspondence with patients in asylums and with their doctors. In 1945 he set out to collect material throughout France and in Switzerland, and in 1947 he opened *Le Foyer de l'art brut* at René Drouin's gallery. The following year the *Compagnie de l'art brut* was founded and the works—now augmented—were transferred to the house of the publisher, Gaston Gallimard.[19] In October 1949 the first public exhibition of *l'art brut* was organized at René Drouin; Dubuffet prepared the catalogue to which he contributed the essay, "L'Art brut préferé aux arts culturels."

This important exhibition listed 200 pieces: paintings, carvings, terracotta sculptures, drawings, manuscripts, embroideries, objects made from—or with—flint, shells, cement, corks, the bark of trees, dolls' heads, sheep's teeth. About half of the objects were made by institutionalized persons and others by inspired craftsmen and artists living in isolation and out of contact with the professional art world. Like folk art, many of the objects showed the seepage downward from past artistic expressions. Even the crude work by a professional artist like Gaston Chaissac, a favorite pupil of the abstract painter Otto Freundlich in Paris, was included.

Yet the collection of *l'art brut* manifests extraordinary originality, and some of the artists, especially Heinrich Anton, Gaston Duf., Auguste For., Miguel Hernandez, Juva, Salingardes, Scottie Wilson, Jeanne le Medium show an obsessive and frightening fantasy, although they seem always to be limited in their vision.

The Desert Track. 1949. Oil emulsion on masonite, $19^3/4 \times 24$". Private collection

Man in the Country. 1949. Oil on canvas, 45$^{1}/_{2}$×34$^{3}/_{4}$". Collection Alfonso Ossorio, East Hampton, New York

45

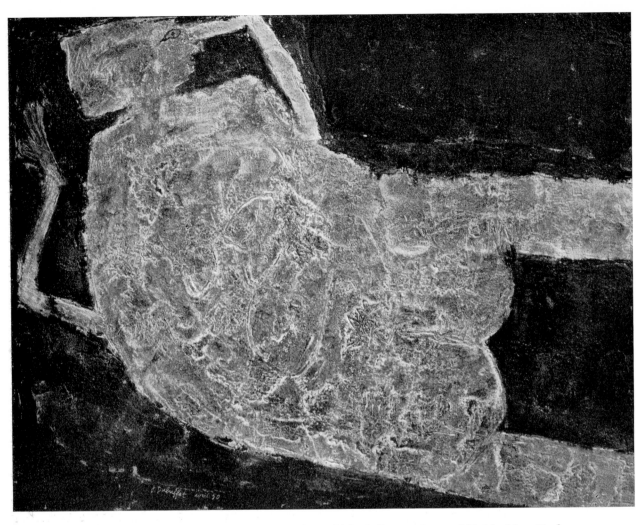

Olympia (Corps de Dame). 1950. Oil on canvas, $35^{1}/_{8} \times 45^{7}/_{8}''$. Collection Larry Aldrich, New York

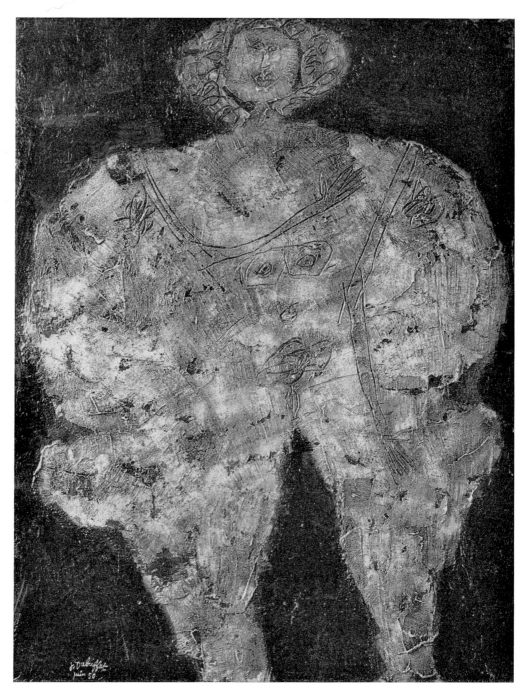

Rose Incarnate (Corps de Dame). 1950. Oil on canvas, 45⁵/₈×35". Collection Alfonso Ossorio and Edward Dragon, East Hampton, New York

More commanding, and also more monstrous, than the *art brut* collection is Dubuffet's next series, his Corps de Dames. The artist's more deliberate control makes for a more universal statement which is not specifically or obsessively tied to some urgent need. And when the element of chance does occur, it is seized upon with a deliberate purpose. Dubuffet speaks of the apparent flaws "which I am inclined to leave in my paintings, for example, the accidental blotches, clumsy blunders, forms that are frankly wrong, anti-real, colors that are unwelcome, inappropriate, all things that would probably seem insufferable to certain people. They even make me a little uneasy because, in many cases, they destroy the effect. But this uneasiness I voluntarily sustain, for it keeps the painter's hand ever present in the painting and prevents the object from dominating and from things taking shape too clearly."[20]

These pictures ironically called Corps de Dames, are surely among the most aggressively shocking works known to the history of painting. By their brutal attack on "Woman" they violate all our sacred and dearly held concepts of mother, wife, mistress, beloved, daughter and sister, as well as the very principles of beauty derived from erotic desire in most cultures. For in their humanness, they far out-distance the "humanism" of the conventional nude in art.[21] The fact that they may vaguely resemble paleolithic sculpture (such as the Venus of Willendorf) or certain Colima terracottas from pre-Columbian Mexico, does little to ameliorate the shock felt before these nudes, especially for those of us brought up within the culture of classical esthetics. The prostitutes of Rouault and Grosz, even Picasso's weeping women of the post-*Guernica* period, leave us unprepared for these deformations.[22]

Cut off at the legs below the crotch, these women with their minute and flattened heads explode laterally to fill the canvas. Some of the bodies are like geographic maps in which schematic signs for arms, breasts, sex, buttocks, thighs, appear as though they were conventional symbols. The arms are sometimes raised to expose a bloated body in which the vulva has become an almost independent object within the carefully charted territory.

They are primordial women, who in all their repulsive brutality speak most revealingly about the human animal, at times satisfied, at times alarming, but always grotesque.

In the earlier paintings of the group, like *Le Metafisyx* or *Olympia* (the irony in this title leaves us incredulous that Manet's perky little nude could have caused a scandal in the Salon of 1865), the body is still quite clearly articulated. These works often evoke images of age-old

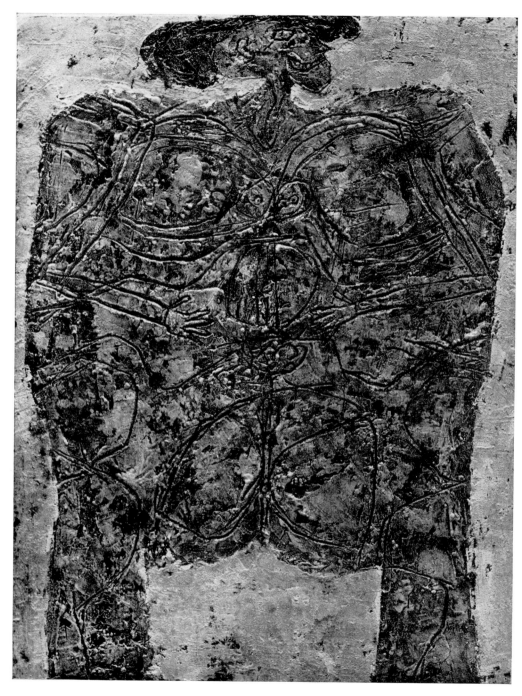

Le Metafisyx (Corps de Dame). 1950. Oil on canvas, 45³/₄×35¹/₄″. Collection Alfonso Ossorio, East Hampton, New York

49

Gaudy Bunch of Flowers (Corps de Dame). 1950. Oil on canvas, 45^{5}/$_{8}$×35″. Sidney Janis Gallery, New York

Corps de Dame. 1950. India ink, 10⁵/₈×8¹/₄". Collection D. B. C.

Corps de Dame. 1950. India ink, 12³/₄×9³/₄". Collection Mr. and Mrs. Walter Bareiss, Greenwich, Connecticut

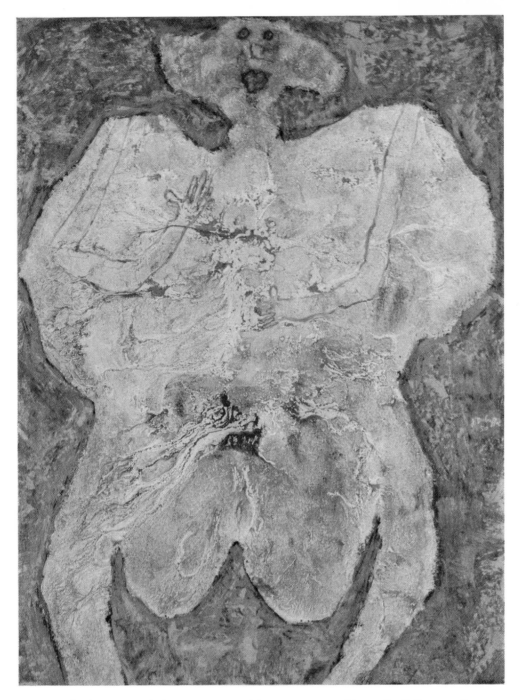

Tree of Fluids (Corps de Dame). 1950. Oil on canvas, 45⅝×35″. Collection Jacques Sarlie, New York

monuments to a female *Erdgeist*. Later, as in *The Tree of Fluids*, he avoids definition of the outline, permitting the body to expand into an almost formless merger with the ground, creating a continuous and pervading flow. "My intention was," he explained, "for the line not to give the figure any definite form, but that it should, on the contrary, prevent the figure from taking a specific shape, so that it would be maintained as a general concept in a state of immateriality."[23]

The material itself is changed from the surfaces resembling chipped rock or earth in the earlier Bodies to the thinner medium used later which somehow suggests a visceral sensation of the body fluids themselves. As always in Dubuffet's work, the picture results from the "dialogue between the artist and his material."[24]

The drawings for the Corps de Dames followed his paintings. Unlike most painters who are likely to begin their visual research with drawings, Dubuffet makes his significant discoveries when fully engaged with tactile materials and then often brings these ideas to their final and more aloof condensations in drawings which, in turn, lead him on to new experiments. The drawings in India ink (there are about fifty), the fifteen lithographs and several gouaches of Corps de Dames are summary sketches on the same theme and use identical imagery, but they have separate identities resulting from the frenzy and quickened rhythm of the linear strokes. A definite hostility to the female body which is apparent in the painting becomes even more evident in the hatched and jagged renderings on paper.

While painting the final canvases of the Corps de Dames, Dubuffet made a small group of wild-looking, flattened-out male figures which resemble handfuls of mud or wet plaster, hurled against a wall, and then worked over with the artist's hands and tools. He certainly felt no more charitably toward these gentlemen; indeed, as proper mates to the ladies, they are entitled Chevaliers. Like some of the ladies, they have a dried-out, crusty appearance and the contours of the bodies are violated by innundations. In their earthlike aspect, they too are territories as well as anatomies (page 56).

Dubuffet constantly shuttles between opposite poles. After working with the thick pastes, he is likely to turn to a thin, fluid medium or to drawing with hard pencils on paper. After long periods of using dark monochromatic materials, he may use vividly colored butterfly wings or he may paste together small, bright pieces of painted canvas as in his assemblages. He will

The Geologist. 1950. Oil on canvas, 38 × 51". Private collection

alternate likewise between joyful and tragic paintings, between figure and landscape and, while still occupied with painting and drawing the bodies of men and women, he examines the surface and structure of the earth.

In December 1950 he painted *The Geologist*, a little man armed with a magnifying glass, walking over the barren crust of the earth, or perhaps on top of a cross-section of geological strata. The soil is seen head-on and simultaneously from the top, but a narrow band of sky still gives us some possibility of orientation. Soon, even sky is eliminated and the total picture surface is covered by a hard impasto forming the relief of the landscape. The little geologist becomes engulfed in the scarred earth: we, the viewer, become, in fact, the geologist as we are offered the surface face-on for investigation. Looking at one of these Sols et Terrains, the observer finds the absence of a visual center—always a principle of Dubuffet's disorganization —more important than ever. There is no direction or orientation in these landscapes expanding before us in four directions. Dubuffet's landscapes are, in fact, more "realistic" than the traditional Western landscapes; and in their boundlessness, homogeneity and extension they also differ from the dispersal of motifs in Chinese landscapes.

Sometimes a few people or animals, roots, primitive implements or rock formations seem to appear. But, since the scale is as ambiguous as the orientation, we may be presented with whole parts of terrestial or lunar petrified continents studded with craters and dry riverbeds. As he continues working on the Sols et Terrains, they become increasingly removed from real places and objects toward "dreamscapes" or—as he says—"landscapes of the mind."

And then—like tablelands—the terrains become tablelike: upturned table-tops whose legs are amputated such as those of the Corps de Dames. These tables are asymmetrical, vague in form, in a state of becoming—or perhaps they are so ancient and worn that all definite outlines have disappeared (pages 58, 70). As man works his land, so he is always accompanied by some sort of surface, a bench or table used for eating and working. There are tables on which the whole history of nature is recapitulated, tables with faces, "quiet tables," "wild tables," or, later, "venerable tables," "bare tables" (page 130), "bestial tables" and "tables of offering."

The landscapes and the tables may also become philosopher's stones, devices for contemplation and echoes of silence, whose encrusted surfaces lead the mind in any direction without stamping upon it certain predetermined shapes. Because, as he ends his poetic essay on this

Knight Attacked. 1951. Oil and various pastes on canvas, 36 × 28³/4″. Collection
Mr. and Mrs. Harry W. Glasgall, New York

Night Frolic. 1951. Oil and various pastes on composition board, 21 × 25¹/₂″. Private collection

series: "The kingdom of formal ideas always appears to me of very little virtue beside the seignioral kingdom of stones"[25] (page 59).

Finally the medium becomes thin and light again, as the sky appears and forms are more clearly defined. These tumultuous and ecstatic skies which now take up the largest amount of space in the vertical Inhabited Heavens are some of the most jubilant paintings in Dubuffet's career (page 61). The Inhabited Heavens were painted during the summer of 1952 after Dubuffet's return to Paris from a six-months' sojourn in the United States. In November 1951 he had come to New York where his work was already fairly well-known and even influential, since it had first been shown at the Pierre Matisse Gallery in 1946. But, in general, Dubuffet's work was difficult to understand and was received unfavorably by critics in both popular and art magazines.[26]

The Museum of Modern Art showed one of Dubuffet's paintings, *Snack for Two*, in its Recent Acquisitions show in 1948, and his work was also exhibited at the Kootz Gallery in addition to his regular shows at Pierre Matisse. In December of that year he opened his first retrospective exhibition at the Arts Club of Chicago with his famous lecture, *Anticultural Positions*,[27] which gave a very clear exposition of his point of view. His Chicago exhibition had a strong affirmative influence on the development of a number of important painters and sculptors there. Returning to New York, he lived on the Bowery and executed a number of marvelous drawings, the so-called Bowery Bums, whose uneasy figures emerge from the rapid quiver of his scribbled lines.

During his stay in New York he also continued working on the Sols et Terrains, using different materials like Swedish putty (a mixture of plaster, glue and varnish) and a synthetic product called spot putty to achieve hard surfaces having the appearence of dry old skin or cracked red clay. Much of this work done in New York, as well as some of the earlier pictures,

Table of Undefined Form. 1951. Oil and various pastes on composition board, 28³/4×36¹/4″. Collection Roland Penrose, London

Stone of Dordogne. 1952. Oil on masonite, 36 × 48″. Private collection

above: *Landscape with Two Personages*. 1952. India ink, 19³/₄ × 25³/₄″. Collection Mr. and Mrs. Pierre Matisse, New York

Bowery Bum. 1951. India ink, 12¹/₄ × 9″. Collection D. B. C.

Ecstasy in the Sky. 1952. Oil and spot putty on composition board, 45¹/₂ × 35″. Private collection

were shown after Dubuffet's departure in Pierre Matisse's exhibition, "Landscaped Tables, Landscapes of the Mind, Stones of Philosophy," for which the artist wrote an excellent essay.[28] Upon his return to Paris, he continued making Landscapes and Stones with thick impasto before turning to his Skies and to the delicately interlaced drawings, Terres Radieuses (Radiant Lands), where both soil and sky become dematerialized into bizarre linear networks in which small human beings are enmeshed, or which are simply calligraphic equivalents of organic structure (pages 60, 75).

Dubuffet has himself discussed his various series beginning in 1951. His writings are never theories illustrated by his work; instead, they are always derived from it, for he becomes aware of his ideas during the very act of painting. He writes clearly and persuasively, betraying the early training of the ubiquitous lycée. Indeed, he is probably the most articulate and lucid artist writing on art since Delacroix and van Gogh. He discusses the materials and tools he uses and his reasons for using them with only a minimum amount of rationalization. It is in his "poetic" passages that his vivid imagery comes into play, as when he is describing the appearance of his own work: "Or else I have given to an insignificant detail . . . enormous and completely arbitrary importance, even to the point of making a legendary hero out of the hairs in the ear. . . ."[29] This is an example of his humor, too, and as in his work itself, he likes to perform sudden, slightly clownish somersaults—to make remarks (particularly at the conclusion of a passage) that have a tongue-in-cheek sound which renders them, as he intends, especially memorable.

In the *Memoir*, included here (pages 73–138), he often repeats himself. It is hoped, however, that this repetition may deepen and broaden the understanding of the artist's thinking and working process, largely because Dubuffet's lively and varied style makes a kind of theme-and-variation out of what is essentially a single thought.[30]

Landscaped Tables, Landscapes of the Mind, Stones of Philosophy
— by Jean Dubuffet

The pictures done in 1950 and 1951 are closely linked, like all my works of these last years, to the specific behavior of the material used, and, if you will, to its disposition. I say its disposition in the sense one speaks of the disposition of an animal, for I should say right off that I see no great difference (metaphysically, that is) between the paste I spread and a cat, a trout or a bull. My paste is a being as these are. Less circumscribed, to be sure, and more emulsified; its ordinance is stranger, much stranger certainly; I mean foreign to us, humans, who are so very circumscribed, so far from the formless (or, at least, think ourselves to be). All the more interesting then, being the bearer of a knowledge to which, without its aid, one could not aspire. Capable of bringing to us astonishing news from the country of the non-circumscribed, from the country of the formless—far better than a cat, or a trout. Those who imagine that these kinds of pastes are something inert make a grave mistake. Formless does not mean inert, far from it! My connection with the material I use is like the bond of the dancer with his partner, the rider with his horse, the fortune teller with her cards. One can now understand how I feel in coming upon a new kind of coating, and with what eagerness I try it out.

I handled for a long time, this year, a paste which I made myself at the time I used it (it dries very quickly); I mixed zinc oxide with a lean but viscous varnish, rich in gum, very much like the one sold in New York under the name of damar varnish. This paste, while still fresh, repels the oil, and the glazes one applies on it organize themselves into enigmatic branchings. Gradually, as it dries, its resistance to the fat colored sauces weakens, and it assembles them differently. Its behavior changes every fifteen minutes.

These branched facts, running trees, by which I saw my figures suddenly illuminated, have transported me into an invisible world of fluids circulating in the bodies and around them, and have revealed to me a whole active theater of facts, which perform, I am certain, on some level of life. Half revealed, of course, in some sphinx's tongue, very different from our articulated languages: one expects such a tongue from a being as different from ourselves as gum-varnish. I must say my feeling is—always has been—very strong that the key to things must not be as we imagine it, but that the world must be ruled by strange systems of which we have not the slightest inkling. This is why I rush towards strange things. I am quite convinced that truth is strange; it is at the far end of strangeness that one has a chance to find the key to things.

Having been attached for such a long time—a whole year—to the particular theme of the body of the naked woman, it was to this theme again that I first linked my experiments with new techniques, and you will find examples in such paintings as *The Tree of Fluids*. When I ask myself what has brought me to this subject, so typical of the worst painting, I think it is, in part, because the female body, of all the objects in the world, is the one that has long been associated (for Occidentals) with a very specious notion of beauty (inherited from the Greeks and cultivated by the magazine covers); now it pleases me to protest against this aesthetic, which I find miserable and most depressing. Surely I aim for a beauty, but not that one. The idea that there are beautiful objects and ugly objects, people endowed with beauty and others who cannot claim it, has surely no other foundation than convention—old poppycock—and I declare that convention unhealthy. I enjoy, at any rate, dissociating, to begin with, this pretense of beauty from any object I undertake to paint, starting again from this naught. Very often this cleaning suffices for the object to emerge suddenly wonderful—as it is in fact, as any object can be. The beauty of an object depends on how we look at it and not at all on its proper proportions. It is my inclination in this direction that has made certain people believe the mood of my art to be bitter. These people have seen that I intend to sweep away everything we have been taught to consider—without question—as grace and beauty; but have overlooked my work to substitute another and vaster beauty, touching all objects and beings, not excluding the most despised—and, because of that, all the more exhilarating. The beauty for which I aim needs little to appear—unbelievably little. Any place—the most destitute—is good enough for it. I would like people to look at my work as an enterprise for the rehabilitation of scorned values, and, in any case, make no mistake, a work of ardent celebration.

Another material—a thick coating composed only of zinc white and carbonate of lime with polymerized oil—has also interested me very much during this same period. This coating allows for a thick impasto that hardens quickly without shrinking, and which, when mixed with sand, as a mortar, lends itself to unexpected reliefs; these, in another way than the branchings I mentioned above, place the subject in a strange light when they happen to play upon things—a human face, for instance—which, in nature, do not present asperities of this

Natural History. 1951. Oil and various pastes on canvas, 57 × 45".
Collection Mr. and Mrs. Ralph F. Colin, New York

65

kind. Painting is based on accepted conventions of transcription (many painters simply use those established by their forerunners; others established new ones for themselves). Many believe that when they make one forget as much as they can these conventions—hiding, as they say in the theater, the puppet strings—they will obtain a stronger effect of real life. But I believe, on the contrary, that it is much more effective to make these conventions constantly apparent, and even to often change them, and put them constantly in question, so as to prevent them from being forgotten. The so interesting mental processes of a man undertaking to paint things and to create life, mysteriously, with his hands—a sort of life to the square root—will be all the more enlightening, I think, if the presence of the painter (and that of his hands) manifests itself more visibly in the work. That is why one will be all the more struck, I think, by paintings in which a larger part is given to facts that unroll themselves inside the mind of the painter as he works—I mean the most specifically mental facts, foreign to the objects he intends to represent, even when these facts are delirious or absurd. I think the resulting discord, far from weakening the grasp on the existence and life of the object represented, will augment it greatly. I think it was in (more or less conscious) obedience to such an idea that I formerly (around 1943) liked to complicate my figures, if not by branchings and reliefs, at least by painting them in garish colors, some more or less justified, others aggressively arbitrary and discordant. I have a vague idea—it haunts me when I paint—that a melange with the discordant and the contrary of life is useful to produce it, as if life could emerge only where forces fight to prevent it.

My mortar, applied with large dull putty knives, enabled me to provoke systems of reliefs in objects where reliefs are least expected, and lent itself, at the same time, to very realistic effects of rugged and stony terrains. I enjoyed the idea that a single medium should have this double (ambiguous) power: to accentuate the actual and familiar character of certain elements (notably in figurations of ground and soils), and yet to precipitate other elements into a world of fantasmagoric irreality, endowing them with an unknown life, borrowed from other worlds than ours—or the same kind of life, but captured on some of its other levels. I am pleased when life itself is questionable in every part of the painting. I am pleased to see life in trouble, going insane—hesitating between certain forms that we recognize as belonging to our familiar surroundings, and others that we do not, and whose voices astonish—giving rise to ambiguous

Rocks and Underbrush. 1952. Oil and various materials on wood, 44⁷/₈ × 59³/₄". Cordier & Warren, Inc., New York

Landscape with a Partridge. 1952. Oil and various pastes on composition board, $31^7/8 \times 35^7/8$". Collection Mr. and Mrs. James W. Alsdorf, Winnetka, Illinois

forms, coming at the same time from both poles. Ambiguous facts have always a great fascination for me, for they seem to me to be located at just those intersections where the real nature of things may be revealed.

Perhaps it was the time I spent in the deserts of White Africa that sharpened my taste (so fundamental to the mood of Islam) for the little, the almost nothing, and, especially, in my art, for the landscapes where one finds only the formless—flats without end, scattered stones—every element definitely outlined such as trees, roads, houses etc., eliminated. Surely I love especially the earth and enjoy places of this sort. But I must say also that a picture, where a painter would have succeeded in producing strongly a presence of life without employing

Landscape in Metamorphosis. 1952. Oil and various pastes on masonite, 36 × 48″. Sidney Janis Gallery, New York

Work Table with Letter. 1952. Oil paint and Swedish putty on composition board, $35^5/_8 \times 47^7/_8''$. The Museum of Modern Art, New York. Gift of Mr. and Mrs. Ralph F. Colin

anything more precise than formless terrain, would be for me very worthwhile; and that is why I always come back to that enterprise. It seems to me the life enclosed in such a picture would be—by being born in such dismalness—more marvelous; and it seems to me also the effect of gasping produced by the mechanisms of the creation of life, in a painting of this kind, would be more intense than in any other, where the artist makes it easy for himself to dodge the difficulty by peopling his work with objects easily recognizable.

I am pleased if the landscapes I have done in this spirit have an uncertain, unsteady scale. So that one may think, depending on one's mood, before the picture entitled *Solitary Places* of a vast expanse of land, or, equally, of a minute particle of earth drawn to scale, or even enlarged. The landscape *The Geologist* [page 54] can, as one desires, represent a surface of terrain— some arid and savage place—or a cross section of sub-soil. Both at the same time. Similarly, the one called *Concretions of the Earth* which seems to me to evoke places inhabited by mice and moles and seen through their eyes.

It was however in the mood of producing things in their true usual aspect that the afore-mentioned landscapes have been painted; while others, made some months later, as *Landscape with Birds, Landscape with Troubled Sky Flown Over by a Swan, Moonrise with Phantoms,* refer to a completely different mood. I wish to enlarge on that. They are no longer—or almost no longer—descriptive of external sites, but rather of facts which inhabit the painter's mind. These are landscapes of the brain. They aim to show the immaterial world which dwells in the mind of man: disorder of images, of beginnings of images, of fading images, where they cross and mingle, in a turmoil, tatters borrowed from memories of the outside world, and facts purely cerebral and internal—visceral perhaps [cf. page 61].

The transfer of these mental sites on the same plane as that of real concrete landscapes, and in such a way that an uncomfortable incongruity is the result (aggravated by the fact that these elements, stripped of materiality, are represented through a heavy medium, with impasto and high reliefs) seems to me an interesting operation. This brewing of two orders supposedly for-eign to one another, the discovery that they are perhaps not so foreign as one had believed, attracts me very strongly.

One will find, among the other paintings that occupied me last year, a fair number of pictures representing only a table—sometimes loaded with half-determined objects, but most often bare.

71

These tables are treated also with the same mealy and bristling texture as the landscapes, and are related to them. They respond to the idea that, just like a bit of land, any place in this world (especially if it relates to an object so inseparable and so cherished a companion as is a man's own table) is peopled with a swarm of facts, and not only those which belong to the life of the table itself, but also, mixing with them, others which inhabit the thought of man, and which he impresses on the table looking at it. I am convinced that any table can be for each of us a landscape as inexhaustible as the whole Andes range; and, for this reason—every place, for my eyes, being equal to every other—I see little use in traveling. I must say I have all my life always loved tables.

One will find also, among these pictures, certain ones called Stones of Philosophy, which represent only a large stone. These come from the idea, expressed before, that the movements of the mind, if one undertakes to give them body by means of painting—and particularly when it is done in the ways of such a material substance as these heavy pastes—have something in common—are close relatives perhaps—with physical concretions of all sorts, as if there were not there two different orders, but rather two different modes of the same order, with possibilities of all combinations from one to the other [page 59].

It appeared to me that the facts—the pure and simple facts—presented by the form and the texture of these big stones, could make of these pictures, at least with time, companions to which one could become strongly attached. That they should be capable of taking, in certain cases, the function of supports on which one can crystallize one's thoughts, as does the grain of sand on which the oyster makes its pearl. I am struck by the high value, for a man, of a simple permanent fact, like the miserable vista on which the window of his room opens daily, that comes, with the passing of time, to have an important role in his life. I often think that the highest destination at which a painting can aim is to take on that function in someone's life. And it seems to me that it will do it more readily if it is summary, effaced, close to the formless, and if it presents nothing but facts in their purity, and no formal ideas above all. The kingdom of formal ideas always appears to me of very little virtue beside the seignioral kingdom of stones.

Translated by the artist and Marcel Duchamp
Published by Pierre Matisse Gallery, New York, 1952

Memoir on the Development of My Work from 1952 – *by Jean Dubuffet*

TERRES RADIEUSES *(Radiant Lands). Line Drawings in India Ink*
December 1951 to October 1952

In September 1952 the long series of works done with plastic paints put on in a thick paste that was more like putty than paint, draws to an end. As the title Sols et Terrains indicates, they suggested landscapes and led me along parallel lines to Stones of Philosophy and Landscaped Tables. In the last paintings of this series, the skies had overrun a large part of the pictures, sometimes having the appearance of a network comprised of innumerable oscillations (related to the effects obtained in the line drawings called Terres Radieuses), at other times ground into thick stony bits like the soil itself, and again taking the form of heavy draperies dramatically stirring, as in *Exaltation of the Sky* or *Tumult in the Sky* [cf. page 61].

Chronologically, the series of drawings called Terres Radieuses should be situated immediately after the series of paintings called Sols et Terrains. There are forty of these India ink drawings, done either with a pen or with a calamus (a sharpened reed the Arabs use instead of metal pen points). They originated with the idea of reviving the same effects as those produced by the triturations in Sols et Terrains, but this time by means of line drawings without the use of reliefs.

The first drawings of this series had been done in New York, in December 1951 and January 1952, or thereabouts, either with or without watercolor. One of them (not colored) was reproduced in the invitation to the exhibition of the paintings entitled, "Landscaped Tables, Landscapes of the Mind, Stones of Philosophy," at the Pierre Matisse Gallery in New York, February 1952. The six or eight drawings (colored) done in New York at the beginning of 1952, each representing a person, often holding a glass and intended to suggest the Bowery bums, should be considered as belonging to this series, as well as the drawing, *Portrait with Developments* [page 74] also belonging to this New York period.

However, the drawings *Landscape with Two Personages, Liaisons et raisons* [pages 60, 75] and others of the same period, mark certain changes. Everything about them seemed to indicate, I think, a different orientation from that of the paintings in the series Sols et Terrains. They certainly showed a distinctive character which might be called psychic or metaphysical or suggest mental derangement (I had originally given the title Paysages Mentaux [Mental Landscapes] to all these paintings), but intimately related to the exorbitantly heavy triturations, exorbitantly "material" one might say, both in technique and in the subjects evoked (stones, muddy earth, etc.). In fact, it was this close association of very heavily material allusions with those, on the contrary, entirely mental and incorporeal, that gave these paintings their significance. In the first drawings of the series Terres Radieuses, and particularly in those done in New York in December 1951 and January 1952, the same spirit will be found, I believe. But

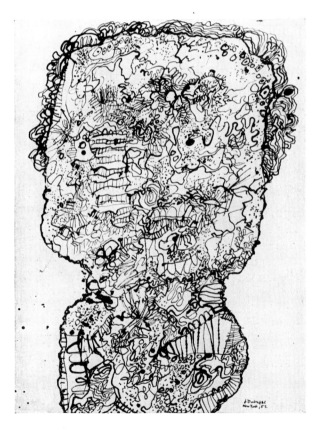

Portrait with Developments. 1952. India ink, 18⁷/₈ ×14¹/₈". Collection D. B. C.

74

with those I did in Paris beginning June 1952, it seems to me the mood changes. It is true that the technique—pen and ink line drawing—naturally led me to less heavily material realizations than in the case of the paintings where I made use of thick pastes. But technique was certainly not alone in giving these new works an entirely different aspect. Instead of making one think of heavy soils like the pictures before them, they suggested extremely light and immaterial elements, such as fine lace, hoar frost and filigrees. Certainly, with this series, a de-corporealizing wind, a wind to sweep everything onto an immaterial psychic plane, now begins to blow through my work and will continue to blow through subsequent series for some years to come.

Liaisons et raisons. 1952. India ink, 20 × 25⅝". Collection D. B. C.

Woman with Red Hat Taking a Walk. 1953. Oil on canvas, 44³/₄ × 57¹/₂″. Private collection

PERSONNAGES PEU CORPOREL ET LIEUX MOMENTANES *(Vaguely Corporeal Personages and Momentary Places). October 1952 and following months*

I remember very well how at this period, after concentrating for so long on paintings in high relief, I now became possessed by the idea of finding a means of expression that would no longer depend on thickness and relief, that would moreover make use of a greater variety of colors, brighter than those rather earthy and monochrome ones in the paintings of the past two years.

These paintings were evolved from various techniques, changing frequently, but in almost all of them occurred colors doused in turpentine, and splashed over fresh oily materials. The result was a whole play of spots and meanders and a breaking up of the surfaces into subtle designs interpenetrating each other.

After drying for a few days there would appear in those paintings in which too much oil had been used and in the places where an excess was concentrated, those wrinkles and curlicues which one ordinarily tries to avoid but which I, on the contrary, undertook to make use of and to provoke in the pictures that followed the ones just mentioned. Returning to the paintings a few days later, when the skin of the surface was beginning to dry and crack, I would tear away with a knife portions of this superficial layer, obtaining effects that resembled abraded skin. This held my attention for a certain time.

PATES BATTUES *(Beaten Pastes). March 1953 and following months*

There is of course something arbitrary about grouping paintings in series, for there are always intermediary zones, and many paintings belong partly to one series, partly to another, and derive from both. It also happens at times that I find myself resorting to a technique belonging to some previous period and take a notion to use it again. This is true moreover not only of the technique but of the mood of a painting, the mood being always closely related to the technique.

Among the works done in the course of the year 1953 will be found not only paintings characteristic of the series known as Pâtes Battues, but numerous others that belong rather to the group, Lieux momentanés of 1952, already mentioned, or others which have something both of Pâtes Battues and of Lieux Momentanés. There will even be found, though more and more rarely, paintings done with thick paste, which should really be grouped with Sols et Terrains.

However, among these paintings of 1953 not readily assignable to any one series, there are a certain number which, by reason not only of their technique but also of their mood and general aspect, add a new and intrinsic element. For this reason I chose to bring them together in a special group under the name of Pâtes Battues for the exhibition at the Cercle Volney.

These paintings are done with a smooth light colored (almost white) paste, fairly thick, spread unevenly and rapidly with a plasterer's knife over layers already thickly painted and still fresh, in such a way that the various colors underneath show where the paste is missing, as well as tint the paste here and there. Then rudimentary figures, hastily traced with a round knife cutting into the paste, play over the surface like graffiti, the variously colored strokes corresponding to the generally dark colors of the previously painted layers. I derived a curiously keen satisfaction from these designs cut into the paste (this white paste, ordinary pigment so finely ground as to resemble butter, gives them a lively subtle character). I am not sure whether this was due to the delicately shaded colorations they made visible, or to the way they seem to record the hasty character of the hand's movements (to me very eloquent). Then finally with a large brush I once more applied (but this time over all the layers) a few colors which blended and blurred all the rest. I am at a loss to explain just what it was in these paintings that gave me—that still gives me—such a keen satisfaction. It has probably something to do with the physical pleasure derived from spreading freely, with a large spatula as broad as one's hand, this beautiful white paste, dazzling and consistent, over a ground previously covered with dark colors, and then letting the long knife with rounded end wander over the smooth paste, tracing with such perfect ease graffiti of sonorous colors. It is the same pleasure that guides the hand of anyone who traces a very hasty design or a word in the fresh plaster of a wall or the freshly smoothed cement of a floor. The hasty uncontrolled character of the resulting design in my picture affords me acute pleasure. I get a feeling of satisfaction from the rough and rudimentary character that this hasty drawing gives to the objects I wish to evoke—the lines intentionally drawn to indicate the presence of some object are often indistinguishable

Still Life with Passport. 1953. Oil on canvas, 38¹/₄ × 51″. Collection Mr. and Mrs. Albert A. List, Byram, Conn.

from those that result from the rapid application of the paste and its "misses," so that the enveloping indefiniteness bathes the whole picture in a kind of ambiguity. Indeed far from keeping me from successfully evoking the subject I set out to represent, this ambiguity actually helps more in this respect than if the objects were clearly defined. It would seem that my obsession for representing things only in a rudimentary and uncertain manner forces the imagination of the person looking at the painting to function more vigorously than it would if the objects were more precisely represented, to such a degree that everything appears to his imagination, thus violently stimulated, with unaccustomed intensity.

The manner in which the lines are briskly cut into the light colored (almost white) paste with a palette knife relates this series of paintings to my Paysages Grotesques of 1949, which made use of the same technique. I might also point out that the designs which appear so rudimentary and careless, so suggestive of the hurried, almost uncontrolled hand that traced them, are to be found in almost all my works since 1942, and constitute perhaps their most significant feature. And I must say that this hasty, loose and very abbreviated manner of transcription affords me a persistent pleasure which I am still unable to explain. Perhaps it is because the objects thus transcribed in hasty strokes succeed for that very reason in constituting a system of signs, a kind of hieroglyphics, very much like rapid, almost automatic writing. The result is a transference from the physical world onto a semi-ideological plane—that of writing—being first very de-corporealized, then re-corporealized later by means of the heavy materials used (thick pastes spread on with big tools). It is as though in a kind of loop-the-loop, the picture made you see at one and the same time all the objects stripped of their flesh and refleshed again with a concentrate of matter no longer appropriate to each separately but borrowed from some more general and indeterminate register and thrown over them all indiscriminately.

I also want to say a word about the particular way the color is distributed in Pâtes Battues. It is done in exactly the same spirit as the designs, that is to say, precipitately and without the least care for precision, not only in the manner in which the colors (those of the objects supposedly) are dashed on in great haste and with no attention paid to putting them in the right places, but there is also confusion (just as there was in the case of the designs) between the colors put on advisedly and those that are where they are by chance. The colors applied with great sweeps of a large brush at the completion of the work are very similar to those which I had spread over the canvas in the first place, before covering them with white paste. These first colors blend, as I have said, on all sides in lovely resonant flashes through the interstices and the "misses" of this sheet of white paste, with no very clear distinction between the emerging colors thus diffused throughout the painting and those applied later on in certain places to define the objects the painting evokes. It should also be added that the colors chosen are few in number with something simplified and arbitrary about them, as if the same free and easy laxness with which they are applied had also been the chief factor even in their choice.

In short, whether it is a question of the manner in which the objects are placed (without perspective and in such a way that the planes that are supposed to be horizontal are scarcely distinguishable from those that are supposed to be vertical, some of the objects having been represented as if seen from above, others as if seen in profile), or whether it is a question of the actual drawing of these objects, or of the colors used and the way they are applied, there is one characteristic common to all the elements of the painting, that is an effect of extreme neglect, of extremely lazy negligence. I feel that to be plunged into this bath of lazy vision and lazy transcription, the world of objects evoked takes on a marvelous power of enchantment, and besides, a power of intense upheaval, of intensified appearance, for the viewer's imagination. However, it is very possible that these effects are an entirely personal matter and function for me alone. In that case the people, and they are numerous, who see in them only an attempt (to them inexplicable) to imitate the drawings that children scribble on walls, would be quite right in finding them devoid of any power at all.

If I have dwelt at length on the paintings of this series, Pâtes Battues, it is because they seem to me, after the long detour of Sols et Terrains, to represent a return to moods that are more or less latent in all my works, and which have kept reappearing in them with insistence. Indeed, all that I have said here about Pâtes Battues applies equally to the series of India ink drawings (with the paper partly abraded) done in 1944, to the Portraits of 1946–47, to Paysages Grotesques of 1949 and Corps de Dames of 1950, etc. . . . .

In all my works, as I realized recently, I have always had recourse to one never varying method. It consists in making the delineation of the objects represented heavily dependent on a system of necessities which itself looks strange. These necessities are sometimes due to the inappropriate and awkward character of the material used, sometimes to the inappropriate

The Busy Life. 1953. Oil on canvas, $51^1/4 \times 77''$. Owned by the artist

manipulation of the tools, sometimes to some strange obsessive notion (frequently changed for another). In a word, it is always a matter of giving the person who is looking at the picture a startling impression that a weird logic has directed the painting of it, a logic to which the delineation of every object is subjected, is even sacrificed, in such a peremptory way that, curiously enough, it forces the most unexpected solutions and, in spite of the obstacles it creates, brings out the desired figuration. I have the impression that the world of objects thus subjected to an extraneous and peculiar logic, appears in an entirely new and unexpected light, so that one sees it with new eyes.

I am convinced, moreover, that one gains by accumulating obstacles, that the more obstacles set up to keep the objects from appearing, the greater the shock when they do appear, just as the rebound of a spring will be all the more violent, the greater the pressure that has been exerted to compress it.

In the case of the works discussed here, the extraneous controlling logic imposed on the paintings is that of laziness, negligence, and the headlong haste with which the pictures seem to have been painted.

LE TORRENT, LES PAPILLONS (*The Mountain Torrent, The Butterflies*). *August 1953 and following months*

In July 1953, having had occasion to drive for a long time along a road in Savoy that followed the course of a mountain torrent, I was seized with a desire to produce something in paint that would have to do with the stony beds of these running waters and the movement of these waters rushing over the stones. The idea of painting water interested me keenly, though I had no conception of how I was going to set about it. A few weeks later I returned to the same region armed with albums and colors in order to study the subject from life. I stayed in the mountains for several days making numerous drawings and watercolor sketches of this torrent with the idea of using them later as memoranda when I returned to Paris and began to work on my project. Meanwhile, my friend Pierre Bettencourt, who had come with me, was catching butterflies. Later he affixed the wings to pieces of paper with a drop of glue

The Butterfly Man. 1953. Butterfly wings and watercolor on cardboard, 9³/₄×7¹/₄". Collection Mr. and Mrs. Donald J. Vlack, New York

and completed the design with watercolors, making little pictures that represented faces. These little pictures composed with butterfly wings fascinated me and made me anxious to try the same method myself.

After this brief stay in Savoy, I painted three large pictures of my mountain torrent. But, as they failed to satisfy me, I put off to a later date the realization of my plan to paint running water. This project with others (for example that of painting ocean water) has preoccupied my thoughts ever since.

Disappointed in the mediocre result of my three attempts to paint my mountain torrent (the paintings are still in my studio waiting for me either to revise them some day or to destroy them), I once more set off for the mountains, this time to chase butterflies. I returned to Paris with an ample collection, and worked steadily for several weeks completing twenty little paintings made with their wings.

ASSEMBLAGES D'EMPREINTES *(Imprint Assemblages). December 1953*
 and following months

The effects I had obtained by my method of making imprints on lithographic paper led me to try the same method with India ink on ordinary paper, beginning in December 1953. An initial series of about twenty little compositions in black and white, approximately the size of a postcard and intended as Christmas cards for my friends, was soon followed by about forty other larger ones done in January and February 1954, and twenty or thirty more in March and April. It should be noted that some of them were completed in a single operation with nothing

84

glued on afterwards and therefore, though looking alike in every respect, cannot be called Assemblages d'Empreintes.

I must also record that it gave me great pleasure to find, possibly for the first time, in certain of the first of these Assemblages d'Empreintes in India ink, effects that seemed to me almost exactly equivalent to the effects produced in preceding years in Sols et Terrains, this time obtained by means of pen and ink alone.

To these same months of January and February 1954 belong a few paintings in gouache, often on black paper, in which I often used imprints done in the same way, and sometimes collage, besides a few pictures composed by assembling torn fragments of newspaper and pasting them together, some of them first maculated with imprints in India ink.

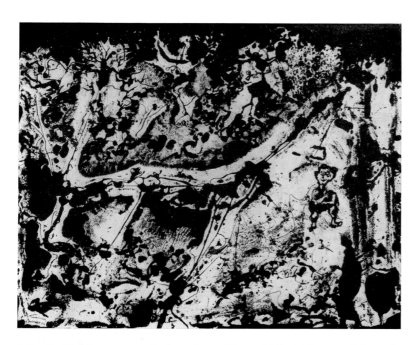

Man in Field. 1953–54. India ink, 19¹/₂ × 25¹/₂″. Collection Mr. and Mrs. Irving Richards, New York

Man with Raincoat. 1954. Assemblage with newspapers, 30³/₄ × 20¹/₂″. Private collection

QUELQUES PEINTURES *(A Few Paintings). January and February 1954*

I am perfectly conscious of the fact that I am drawn simultaneously and alternately to opposite poles. I feel an attraction for outlines defined in the most arbitrary and imperative fashion indicating excessive *intervention* (even though later, as I had mentioned, I drown them in a bath of shadow that obliterates them almost entirely, leaving only indistinct traces); but at the same time I feel a strong inclination to avoid using any outlines at all in a painting, any element of design, any definite lines (whether done with a brush or incised) anything of a graphological nature, so that only the patches of color are allowed to function, interpenetrating each other and forming, through the accidental spread of oil, tortuous and uncertain boundaries which delight me. The only kind of delimitations I want in my picture is that of the boundaries between neighboring patches of color. Instead of an excessive intervention, here we have the exact opposite, an excessive absence of intervention.

Furthermore, even in the choice of colors I am torn by a double attraction, tempted on the one hand to use brilliant, crude colors, arbitrary, blithely false, irrational, preposterous—either

Prompt Messenger. 1954. Oil on canvas, 32×39¹/₂″. Collection Mr. and Mrs. David M. Solinger, N. Y.

by their excessive richness or by their excessive poverty—and, on the other hand, very dull and neutral ones like real colors, such as those of tea, wood, earth, and of the greater part of the things before our eyes, thus also in the realm of color avoiding invention and intervention.

Finally, and this shows how in everything I struggle between two opposite tendencies, although I have a great liking for a picture made with heavy materials suggesting different kinds of mud, and for this reason am often inclined to use paint thickly and in relief, I take just as keen a pleasure in a picture composed of sheets of glaze, very fluid and transparent and as smooth as glass.

As I have already mentioned, after my long session with Sols et Terrains, I was very anxious to find a new means of expression that would exclude the use of relief entirely. I was also anxious to get away from the register of ochres and browns, used persistently throughout Sols et Terrains, to the brilliant fantastic colors of precious stones, and also from the opaque mud colors to those that are translucent and transparent. This was the mood that already prevailed (at least in the Ciels) in the last paintings of the series Sols et Terrains. The series Pâtes Battues, in which I continued to use bright specious colors, but reverted to rather thick pastes, together with the following series derived from these Pâtes Battues, in which reappeared widely dispersed, rather dark colors (but now *shadowy* rather than *earthy*), constituted a long double detour. After this I went back to the point from which I had departed.

PETITES STATUES DE LA VIE PRECAIRE *(Little Statues of Precarious Life)*.
   March to October 1954

The first of these statues was *Grouloulou*, made of pieces of newspaper smeared with glue and bunched around an armature. It was above all a glorification of newspaper paper. I had only recently used torn fragments of newspaper in several of my assemblages, notably in the poster for my show at the Cercle Volney. *Grouloulou* was therefore closely related to these works.

The second was *Gigoton* made of steel wool such as housewives use to clean their pots and pans.

The third, *Personage with Paste Eyes*, made use of fragments of burned automobiles that I found in the garage where I kept my car.

The Ragged One. 1954. Clinker, 28″ high. Collection Mr. and Mrs. Gordon Bunshaft, New York

opposite left: *The Joker.* 1954. Clinker, 12″ high. Collection Mr. and Mrs. Arnold H. Maremont, Chicago

opposite center: *The Maestro.* 1954. Sponge, 17″ high. Collection Mr. and Mrs. Pierre Matisse, New York

opposite right: *Cursed Gossip.* 1954. Charcoal, 13″ high. Collection D. B. C.

Those that followed were made of broken clinkers put together with cement. First I used clinkers I picked out of the trash cans in the apartment house where I was living, but soon I went out looking for more clinkers, as well as for different kinds of rubbish (old trampled cords, broken glass, big rusty nails) in the railroad yards of Montrouge.

It should be noted that these works borrowed my method of assemblage, and may, therefore, be considered a development of the butterfly-wing collages, of the lithographs made of superposed and glued fragments, and of the Assemblages d'Empreintes.

After using clinkers for two months, I went on to sponges. A wholesale dealer on rue

Monge let me take my pick from a huge pile, all of them grotesque and unsaleable. But what were defects for the trade, were added virtues for me. To these assemblages of pieces of sponge I would sometimes add oakum dipped in glue.

Later I made other little statues out of grapevine stocks collected in Burgundy, and out of pieces of charcoal from a coal dealer in Morvan. Finally, beginning in September, for the last of these little statues, I used scoria, pieces of lava, and volcanic stones picked up in Auvergne.

In October 1954 there was an exhibition of about forty-four of these statues at the Galerie Rive Gauche.

I should like to call particular attention to two or three of the statues which are made of light delicate fragments of shredded sponge, for they, even more than any of the others, are characterized by extreme precariousness and immateriality.

L'Ame du Morvan. 1954. Vine stalks on clinker base, 18¹/₂″ high. Collection Alexandre Vialatte, Paris

opposite page: *The Magician.* 1954. Slag and roots, 43¹/₄″ high. Collection N. Richard Miller, New York

I had decided to experiment with a new technique, based on the almost exclusive use of very fluid industrial paints called "enamel paints," which I had worked with occasionally in the past and which I now wanted to try using alone. To begin with, during the month of July I painted four pictures, each with a personage, among which was *The Fur Hat*.

These particular paints were those quick-drying ones known as "four-hour enamels." Spread over a preliminary layer not yet completely dry, they became decomposed, causing a fine network of fissures and crackles. I took full advantage of this property of theirs.

I should note here that it was at this time that my wife's condition, which had been growing worse for some time, was diagnosed as pulmonary tuberculosis, and she was obliged to leave home for a long stay at Puy-de-Dôme.

A series of thirty paintings followed the four just mentioned. They were painted in the same way with quick-drying paints and made use of the crackles formed on a surface not yet completely dry. I combined these enamel paints with ordinary oil paint and, as they displayed a lively incompatability, the result was a whole set of digitate spots and convolutions which I was careful to provoke and turn to account. In this way all the subjects—sometimes landscapes, sometimes figures—became intricately ornamented.

After, as in *The Extravagant One*, I would often finish the painting with a little brush, a task requiring both time and patience. This underlined the tiny network of small veins and oscillations provoked by the juxtaposition of the two hostile paints.

Earlier in this memoir, speaking of Pâtes Battues, I mention that I like to instigate in a painting, along with the reasons implied by the subject treated and by the objects represented, another altogether different set of reasons (recognizing their absurd and inexplicable character without the least displeasure), which seem to have been granted priority in directing the work, and to which everything else must docilely submit even though the result may give an impression of absurdity. I think my pleasure in confronting a given representation—landscapes, figures or anything else—with a certain set of reasons totally foreign to the representation, is at the origin of my taste for changing techniques and materials. In fact, the very reactions of the material chosen, the particular characteristics of the instruments used, furnish, indeed,

The Fur Hat. 1954. Oil on canvas, 39³/₈ × 31⁷/₈″. Private collection

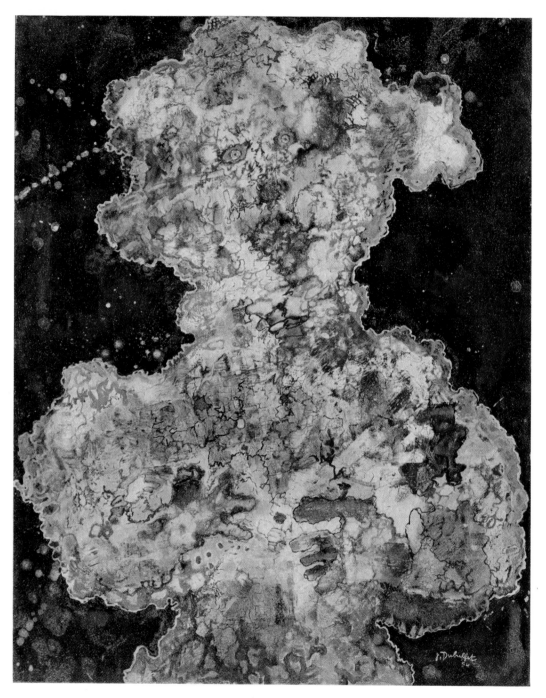

The Extravagant One. 1954. Oil on canvas, 36$^{1}/_{2}$ × 29″. Private collection

The Gypsy. 1954. Oil on canvas, 36¼ × 29". Hillman Periodicals, Inc.

at the very outset, the new set of reasons I am looking for, the new logic in the light of which I like to expose any very ordinary object I happen to think of, which, subjected to this unexpected light, shows unaccustomed and surprising aspects.

In other series of paintings this new polarizing scheme, this initial transmuting device, will be obtained sometimes by the use of an unusual new material (or unusual way of using it) which brings with it its own imperative *reasons*, or, lacking this, by some strange preconceived notion, stubbornly pursued in the manner of evoking the objects, apparently inept and without any valid connection. Later, in the Tableaux d'Assemblages (Painting Assemblages), this strange logic, imposed on the images in the painting, will be found in the reasons (manifestly a bit absurd) inherent in cutting and reassembling.

In the case of the series of paintings here under discussion, the set of reasons which governs the images is to be found in the capricious and complex designs that form by themselves because of the simultaneous use of two kinds of paint with different reactions which combine badly with each other. Later, to accentuate and complete my own organized designs, I deliberately set to work to adopt their language. The result, a whole succession of marbling (small internal branching and intricately embellished surfaces) which succeeds in transporting the subjects of the painting—figure, landscape or anything else—to a world ruled by entirely different reasons, making them appear in an unaccustomed light. In this way, by the revelation of our familiar objects suddenly transformed and strange, is evoked, even quite startlingly sometimes (at least for me), these strange bewildering worlds that exercise a kind of fascination.

VACHES, HERBE, FRONDAISONS *(Cows, Grass, Foliage). Summer 1954*
  and following months

From the beginning of July 1954, as my wife, for reasons of health, was living on the outskirts of Clermont-Ferrand, I often had occasion to drive along the road between Paris and the Auvergne, and to take long solitary walks in the countryside around the village where she was being cared for. In this village I had at my disposal a little place which I fitted up as a studio. Once more I became preoccupied with country subjects—fields, trees, grassy pastures, cattle, carts and the work of the fields—all things I had already treated with enthusiasm in 1943 and 1944. As formerly, I loved spending hours watching the cows and afterwards drawing them from memory, or even, but much more rarely, from life.

Now, a parenthesis. I am obsessed by the idea that there is something both false and un-profitable in looking at things too closely and too long. It is not normal for a human being to stare at objects for the sole purpose of inspecting them and making an inventory of their constituent parts. Such a position in our relation to them seems to me to distort completely (if not to empty them of all content) the mechanisms of communication that exist between man and the objects around him, the way he perceives them and the way they affect him. Man sees things without trying to see them. While he is looking at one thing he sees another as though obliquely, by way of corollary. It is a very curious fact that people who are passion-ately attached to something, say for example to an animal, would not be able to give you any of the animal's exact measurements or else would give incredibly wrong ones, the way children draw from memory objects that are very familiar to them or that have made a deep impression on them. So, it seems to me, that to set oneself to inventory the true measurements of things is a practice without the slightest value. What to me seems interesting is to recover in the rep-resentation of an object the whole complex set of impressions we receive as we see it normally in everyday life, the manner in which it has touched our sensibility, and the forms it assumes in our memory. This is what I have always tried to do. I think that too conscientious a scrutiny of an object distorts the normal mechanism of looking, and I believe that a painter should be very careful to keep himself from over-conscientiousness, should (a very difficult kind of gymnastics) stick to examining and representing things without ever doing violence to that distracted, confused state of mind, that kind of hazy consciousness perpetually in motion, which is man's normal condition when the things around him strike his attention. That is why I have an aversion to drawing any objects from life. Nothing seems to me more false, more stupid, than the way students in an art class are placed in front of a completely nude woman standing motionless on a table, and stare at her for hours. The normal conditions under which a man has seen unclothed bodies are thus disregarded in a perfectly insane fashion, and insane too is the idea that under such conditions anyone could possibly reconstruct anything resembling the image of a naked woman as it exists normally in an ordinary man's memory.

The Spotted Cow. 1954. Oil on canvas, 35 × 46". Collection Mr. and Mrs. Gordon Bunshaft, New York

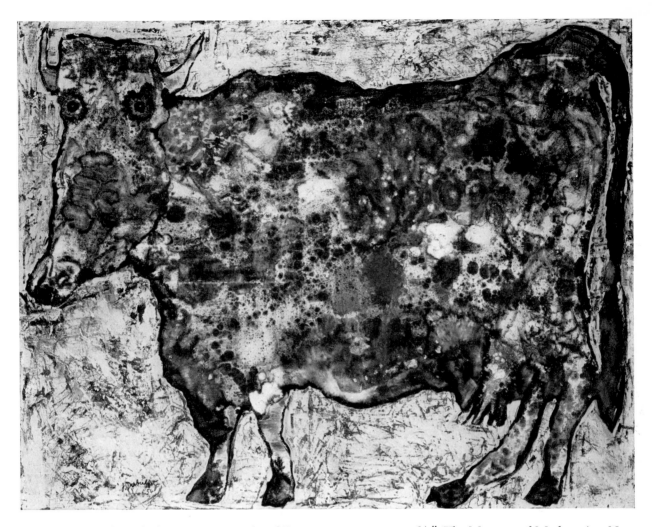

The Cow with the Subtile Nose. 1954. Oil and Duco on canvas, 35 × 45³/₄". The Museum of Modern Art, New York. Benjamin Scharps and David Scharps Fund

Cow with Red Eyes. 1954. Oil on canvas, 31 × 39″. Collection Mr. and Mrs. Albert A. List, Byram, Connecticut

The Cow with Fine Teats. 1954. Oil on canvas, $51^{1}/_{2} \times 38''$. Collection Mr. and Mrs. Harry Sherwood, Los Angeles

It is certainly in the spirit I have just indicated that I have always tried to represent any object, transcribing it in a most summary manner, hardly descriptive at all, very far removed from the actual objective measurements of things, making many people speak of children's drawings. Indeed, my persistent curiosity about children's drawings, and those of anyone who has never learned to draw, is due to my hope of finding in them a method of reinstating objects derived, not from some false position of the eyes arbitrarily focused on them, but from a whole compass of unconscious glances, of finding those involuntary traces inscribed in the memory of every *ordinary* human being, and the affective reactions that link each individual to the things that surround him and happen to catch his eye. As a matter of fact it is difficult to paint objects without deviating from this coveted state of mind, the only one which seems to me valid and without which for me a work is totally devoid of interest. By this I mean that state of seeing things without really looking at them, without paying more attention to them than an ordinary man would in normal life. In this way the subsequent drawing will show the appearance of the objects as they have been impressed on the man's brain when his attention or consciousness did not intervene, or at least intervened only vaguely, or not more than in the daily life of any ordinary man, who is normally preoccupied with all sorts of other things at the moment his eyes light upon any object. It is difficult, I repeat, not to spoil this state of semi-inattention, of hazy consciousness, at the moment one sets oneself to transcribe all the processes and mechanisms resulting from the sight (or evocation in the mind) of a certain object, just as they proceed from that inattentive state of mind itself, and to transcribe what happens to the object in the operation. It therefore becomes a matter of paying great attention to inattention, to being very attentive in transcribing, as skillfully and faithfully as possible, what happens to an object when one sees it without paying much attention. One is inclined to conclude that the method of drawing as taught in art schools can only add to the natural difficulties of such an enterprise, and that the only successful results will be found among completely ingenuous individuals, such as children or those persons who have never taken lessons, but who like idly to trace a design, with a stick perhaps, in the wet plaster of a wall. They are the ones who arouse my curiosity because their performance is only half conscious.

I have dwelt at length on this program for the representation of objects looked at casually, because I believe that it is the mainspring and the constant motive of all my works.

I shall now come back to the cows. First of all I should say that the sight of this animal gives me an inexhaustible sense of well-being because of the atmosphere of calm and serenity it seems to generate. I can also say that pastures, and even merely the color green—because of the cows, I suppose, by an unconscious association of ideas—has a comforting and soothing effect on me. I wonder if people who are especially subject to anxiety and restlessness experience a happy feeling of relief at the sight of green pastures?

But this was not always the effect I wanted to produce. Very often I liked to portray the cow as a kind of preposterous Punch, and to use all the elements of the countryside—meadows, trees and others—to create a sort of grotesque theater, a circus of clowns. This was probably the consequence of the same attitude evident in Portraits, in Arabs, in Corps de Dames or in Paysages Grotesques. It follows the same principle I spoke of in the beginning of this memoir, that of setting up more and more obstacles to prevent the objects from being recognized, in order that finally their presence should come as a shock. Although I never consciously thought of it at the time, on looking back I am sure that in transferring their image to a devil-may-care, arbitrary, phantasmagoric world of clowns, I had an obscure idea of conferring on them, by means of irreality, a more intensely alive reality. After all, this is the aim that is sought, and in the best instances attained, in all good clown acts, in all good theater.

The first of these cows, painted in August and September 1954, borrow the enamel-paint technique already described. The ones done in the following months (the last ones in December) and, in fact, also the paintings on other subjects done at that time, were painted not with enamel paint but with ordinary oil paints.

SECONDE SERIE D'ASSEMBLAGES D'EMPREINTES (Second Series of Imprint Assemblages). Vence, February 1955 and following months

At the end of January I moved with my wife to Vence, a little town specializing in the treatment of pulmonary disorders that her doctors had recommended. It was difficult to find a suitable place for painting, and as at first I had only a very small studio, I arranged it as a workshop for doing another series of Assemblages d'Empreintes in India ink. These occupied my attention for the months of February and March and intermittently during the following months. Between February and June, I finished a series of thirty-three of these imprints, and added seven more during the course of the summer.

These compositions have various themes, some illustrated by figures, others by landscapes, most of them enlivened by figures as well (*The Lady with a Parasol*). The landscapes for the most part evoke stretches of barren, stony ground, rather ill defined. The figures in them, because of their fantastic delineation, their dancing, leaping attitudes, give the impression of instantaneousness (of the vivid capture of a passing instant) and have, it seems to me, the effect of investing the whole scene around them with a very special atmosphere of enchantment. In these, as in many of my works (I might say in all to them), it will be noticed that I have used a means to this end which might be explained as follows: the fact that certain elements (the figures in the present case) are delineated in a very epitomized and free-and-easy manner tends to release the creative activity of the imagination of the viewer and by this means all the other elements in the picture (those indefinite stretches of earth, for instance) seem to him endowed with a more intense reality and life.

Lady with a Parasol. 1955. India ink (imprint assemblage), 28³/₈ ×18¹/₈". Collection Mr. and Mrs. Joseph Bissett, New York

opposite page: *Walking in the Bushes.* 1954. India ink (imprint assemblage), 19⁷/₈×25³/₄". Collection André Berne-Joffroy, Paris

However, little by little, new themes appear in these assemblages, and will be found again in the paintings of the following months. They are probably connected with all the new sights offered me during my stay in Vence, such as the two-wheeled carts, the varied plant life—with a persistent predilection for an equivocal suspense between the gaiety of a pleasure garden and the forlorn aspect of some untidy spot overgrown with weeds....

All my work with assemblages—not only the ones of this series but also those I did in Paris the year before and the ones I did later both in Vence and in Paris—were not so much undertaken with the idea of realization as in the spirit of preliminary research, with a view to future realizations. In short, they were for me what preliminary sketches of a painting are for other painters. This assemblage technique, so rich in unexpected effects, and with the possibilities it offers of very quickly changing the effects obtained through modifying the disposition of the haphazard pieces scattered on a table, and thus of making numerous experiments, seemed to me an incomparable laboratory and an efficacious means of invention. This said, I admit that

I am often satisfied with imperfect realizations, in a hurry to go on to other experiments, and so put off to a later date developing them with greater application.

It is true that what I have just said about these assemblages in ink applies equally to most of my paintings (perhaps all of them), for they are usually done in the same spirit of research and experimentation, with the idea of developing them more carefully later. This I often fail to do, impatient as I am to go on to other experiments. Besides, I really believe that the hasty and unfinished character of a painting adds to the pleasure it gives me, and I seldom feel that the effects I have sketched need a more meticulous execution.

CHARRETTES, JARDINS *(Carts, Gardens). First Paintings Done in Vence, April to June 1955*

In April 1955, having found a suitable studio in Vence, I could begin painting again. I painted about thirty pictures during the months of April, May, and June.

The first of these paintings, such as *Tourist at a Beautiful Place*, do not seem to me to be worth any special mention as they are products of the same spirit and technique as some of my previous paintings; their mood is that of a *refined primitivism*. The striking colors of the paintings done in Paris previous to these, are now replaced by what might be called natural colors, rather light but stony, earthy, sandy (whites, grays, ochres, gold shades, bistre). One finds the same empirical delineation as in Paysages Grotesques and other earlier paintings. The lines are traced in the paste with the end of a stick, making one think of the drawings one sees scribbled on walls. They are painted with ordinary oil pigments and make a generous use of paste, following pretty closely the technique of the Pâtes Battues of 1953.

Soon, however, I discovered a new process that enriched this technique, and used it more all the time. It consists of making impressions in fresh paste, of various manufactured objects that produce more or less geometrical reliefs, such as cake molds, various household and kitchen utensils, salad baskets, a soap dish, a ribbed rubber mat, sacking with a very large mesh, etc. I began laying in a whole stock of these utensils from the bazaars, hardware stores and department stores of Nice. Moreover, I made use of them again in subsequent works done with India ink. In making some of the imprints of these objects, I returned to the use of thick plastic

Tourist at a Beautiful Place. 1955. Oil on canvas, 31⁷/₈ × 39⁵/₈″. Private collection

My Cart, My Garden. 1955. Oil on canvas, 35×45³/4″. Collection Mr. and Mrs. James Thrall Soby, New Canaan, Connecticut

paints with a base of polymerized oil, which I had not used for some time, but which are better for taking impressions than zinc white, ground with oil.

At the same time that my techniques were changing in the making of these imprints, the themes and the style of the paintings were also taking a new turn. As to the subjects treated, they converged toward a new theme, (already mentioned in connection with the assembled prints) that of pieces of ground planted with growing things—tufts of grass, lowly weeds that look like stars, such as plantains, thistles or dandelions, coming up between little stones in what appears to be the ground on the edge of badly kept roads, or barren mountain soil like the soil around Vence. As to the style of the paintings it is characterized by a minute and copious over-all picturization, provided by a great array of imprints of those utilitarian objects already mentioned, with long meticulous intervening lines done with a fine brush. These lines serve to heighten the effect of stones, thyme, mosses, lichens, but also in unexpected places, to embellish, for example, the zones of bare sky or earth. In this way is realized the double effect of a very descriptive realism as well as an extensive and peacefully delirious unreality, creating between them a provocative ambiguity.

The colors in these paintings are light, quite restrained, and diffuse.

SECONDE SERIE DE PETITS TABLEAUX D'AILES DE PAPILLONS *(Second Series of Little Paintings of Butterfly Wings). Vence, June to September 1955*

Remembering what pleasure I had had in making a series of assemblages of butterfly wings two years before, and being now in a place where, after April, butterflies are plentiful and particularly lovely and varied, I began chasing them again. The liveliness of the chase itself, the exhilarating effect of the hot sunshine of this country, new to me at that time, and the charm of the mountain solitudes where I chased the butterflies, certainly had something to do with my excitement over this work. During the months of June to September, I finished about thirty of these little compositions made of butterfly wings stuck to the paper with a bit of glue, the background tinted with watercolor, and sometimes decorated later with lines put in with a fine brush that suggested the natural nervures of the wings. This was at a period when I was always awakened very early, and I would do this delicate work during the first hours of the morning, leaving the rest of the day free. I still, however, continued as usual with my other work in oil, India ink, and watercolor. Several subjects now held my attention with persistence. At first it was the sun-dried stone walls one sees everywhere in Vence. There was a very beautiful one in front of my house and I spent much time studying it and sometimes making patient pencil sketches. But I was even more fascinated by the tiny botanical world at the foot of the walls, worthless and charming, overrunning the side of the road among little stones, and mixed with the dusty trash that collects along neglected roadways. For two or three months I was much preoccupied with this subject and, carrying a folding stool, a bag slung over my shoulder containing water-bottle, watercolors, and sketchbook, I would betake myself to lovely little roads where I could work undisturbed, or even to the more frequently traveled highways where I was much less comfortable. In either case sitting in front of these tiny spectacles (you don't have to go far to find them, they are everywhere) I would make detailed notes. My subject was a small piece of ground—hardly more than a meter or two—at the side of the road, sparsely gravelled, or perhaps formerly partly covered with asphalt or tar and now slowly disintegrating, while a tiny population of delicate tufts of grass, thistles, and minute plants takes possession of the crevices between the little stones and bits of gravel. Sometimes the stone step at the entrance to houses or gardens, gratuitously surrounded by this humble vegetation, was also the subject of these notes, and I often thought of making it the subject of paintings too (I have not done so yet) because of all that the idea of the doorstep suggest to the imagination.

At the same time, another theme, kindred if you like, yet very different, that of gardens, claimed my thoughts. Vence is largely made up of villas surrounded by gardens, many of them badly kept and running wild. The spectacles offered by these gardens when one looks *up* at them—that is to say, into the trees and masses of foliage—vertical spectacles one might call them—and those that are horizontal looking *down*—that is at the sandy, stony ground, the twigs and dead leaves, the humus, and the tiny plants mixed with little stones (I said the gardens were unkempt) now constituted my subjects. I made detailed, documentary drawings of these also, with the idea that I would think of some way, some ingenious, oblique, round-about method, by which I would be able to reconstitute something equivalent to these spectacles. I must admit, to be exact, that I felt a kind of hesitation in my choice between the vertical and the horizontal appearance of these gardens, not being able to bring myself to connect them

Medieval Garden. 1955. Butterfly wings, 9 × 11¹/₂″. Collection Grant J. Pick, Glencoe, Illinois

The Garden of Bibi Trompette. 1955. Butterfly wings and gouache, 9 × 12¹/₂″. Montgomery Art Center, Pomona College, Claremont, California. Gift of Mr. and Mrs. Norton Simon.

by the ordinary means of perspective which seemed to me to distort their aspect entirely (or at least the affective impression they gave me), taking away all the life and charm of the subject. So my problem (and it is the problem I often encounter in my work) was to find in the disposition of my composition some way of blending the vertical with the horizontal, of mixing them, or of devising in the painting a zone of ambiguity between them.

My simultaneous preoccupation with these two subjects, that of the little plants growing along the roadside and that of the gardens (the first dealing with very small surfaces, the second with larger spaces) resulted in some confusion between them. This ambiguity, as a matter of fact, gave me a certain pleasure, and I had no objection to seeing my images straddling the two subjects, somewhat equivocally evoking both at the same time, and providing an occasion for musing on the tenuous and somewhat absurd character of the trouble man takes to plant these gardens which are so soon victoriously taken over by unbridled Nature, and also for wondering at the sumptuous richness and variety of one small square meter of cracked asphalt where bits of grass are growing. It pleased me to confound the difference in scale between the two.

To come back to my butterflies. It was inevitable that my compositions of assembled butterfly wings, done at a moment when my mind was full of these themes, should bear upon them too. And that is exactly what happened. It is true that there were also a few fantastic, extravagant personages born of these assemblages of wings, but the greater part of the compositions represented gardens in the more or less equivocal fashion I have described.

This new series of assemblages of butterfly wings was a determining factor in my later works. The very material used (altogether unusual) and the play of the nervures, added a strange irreality to the paintings, but a compelling authority as well, due to the impression it gave of cohesion, of necessity, of an inexplicable but very impelling logic, that *set of reasons* foreign to the reasons of the objects themselves, which I spoke of in an earlier chapter. I kept a nostalgic feeling for these mechanisms, with the persistant idea of finding later on some equivalent in my paintings.

In addition, the particular constitution of the color in these assemblages of butterfly wings affected me strongly. I had plenty of time, while adding watercolor around the wings in order to bind them together and to create an effect of masses, to notice that the colors of butterflies are not really very vivid, as generally supposed, but delicate and lustrous; and the over-all color of my little paintings was pearly, iridescent, and one sensed a subtle sheen rather than color in the real sense of the word, a scintillation that I would afterwards stubbornly try to get in my paintings.

In the month of July 1955, I painted with great care four large pictures imitating four of my butterfly-wing compositions. They were like enlargements, scarcely transformed at all. It was just slavish copying and naturally of very little interest, but I mention it here simply to show to what an extent I was interested in the effects I had achieved by means of these assemblages of butterfly wings. Only very much later I was to find at last (with great pleasure) satisfying equivalents in my Tableaux d'Assemblages.

PERSONNAGES MONOLITHES *(Monolithic Personages). Vence, July to October 1955*

While I worked on my little butterfly-wing pictures, and intermittently on documentary drawings and watercolors of the rough surfaces of bad roads, and of the tiny grasses and plants growing in the ditches, I continued at the same time with my paintings. At first I treated these same subjects (*The Prowling Dog*), representing a dog wandering over ground covered with vegetation, a good example of the bridge between the theme of the Garden and that of the humble vegetation growing wild. Then I did some paintings of people but soon these took a very different turn. This was the result of a new technique that I afterwards used abundantly, and consisted in applying large newspaper sheets to fresh paint. The paintings were begun in the same way as the Pâtes Battues, a technique I kept going back to, that of spreading with a spatula a very light (almost white) brilliant color generously over layers (dry or partly dry) of different dark shades, the paint often thickly laid on. But now, over this fresh white paste, I spread various other shades, once more using strong colors and, without letting them dry, I applied whole newspapers, generally folded perpendicularly or sometimes intentionally crumpled. This operation removed a great deal of the color of the last layer, leaving only spots and flashes arranged in a curious and interesting fashion (with marks left by the folds of the news-

The Prowling Dog. 1955. Oil on canvas, $32\frac{1}{2} \times 39\frac{3}{8}$″. Private collection

paper). Finally with a large soft brush I spread a background of black paint, leaving, however the outlines of a person, or more often two, making two figures appear side by side. The indefinite blurred contours of the figures I had formed, and the way they stood out so startlingly white against the black background, made them look like menhirs. All I had to do then was to finish off the figures lightly with a brush, taking care not to make my interventions too precise and so spoil the character to which they owed their special effect, that of stone figures born of circumstances almost foreign to the original intentions, rising all at once and instantaneously formed.

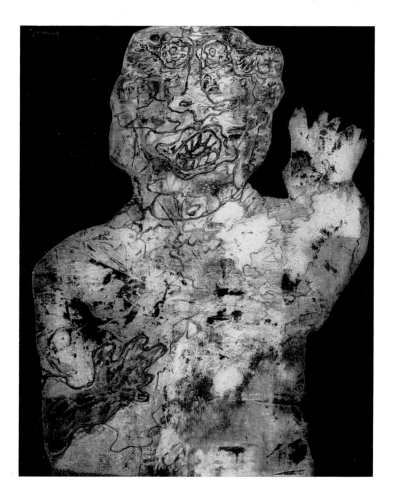

Artful Hubbub. 1955. Oil on canvas, 36¹/₄ × 28³/₄″. Collection
Mr. and Mrs. Herbert Ferber, New York

TABLEAUX D'ASSEMBLAGES *(Painting Assemblages). November 1955 and following months (until mid-December 1956)*

After composing my assemblages of India ink imprints I was anxious to try the same technique in my oil paintings. I looked forward to making all sorts of experiments with different textures, spots, maculations, etc., cutting out the parts that pleased me, and assembling them as I chose. I was interested in such a technique principally because it allowed me to make my initial spotting with greater freedom, unrestrained by the fear of spoiling the rest of the painting. In my previous works I had indeed always preferred a daring, hazardous way of painting, with the idea of provoking all sorts of accidents more or less deliberately, but not easily controlled. With such methods, however, I had to be careful to respect the design or at least the subject (though often lured into changing the design and even the subject of the painting when inveigled by these accidents of execution), always hampered by the fear that the daring maneuver destined to improve one part of the painting should turn out to have spoiled others, and often a happy accident would occur but not in the spot where it was wanted. My new project would allow me to make all sorts of experiments without ever having to be careful. I would be able also to make any number of experiments on fragments of any dimension cut from a roll of canvas according to my needs, without the necessity of stretching rectangles on frames. If it were a question, let us say, of representing an object on a table, I could paint the table separately, the object separately, or make various different sketches of the object and then try the effect of one on the other by simply pinning them for a moment on to a board. Then too I could add as I chose other elements to the picture, or later even incorporate the whole painting in a larger one, and there would be no limit to whatever might occur to me in the way of additions or enlargements.

Technical problems retarded somewhat the execution of this project. The first problem was to find the proper glue. At first I thought I had found it in the one recommended by art restorers. It necessitated a whole arsenal of presses, which I constructed. But in the end it proved to be insufficiently strong so that I had to take the pictures I had done apart and glue the pieces all over again, using a new glue, with a latex base that shoe manufacturers use for gluing

The Gardens of the Highway. 1956. Oil on canvas (assemblage), 49¹/₄ × 39″. Private collection

opposite: *I Live in a Happy Country*. 1956.
Oil on canvas (assemblage), 57$^{1}/_{2}$×37$^{1}/_{2}$″.
Private collection

Astravagale. 1956. Oil on canvas (assemblage), 28$^{3}/_{4}$×17″. Collection G. David Thompson, Pittsburgh

leather. Having put it to the test, I think by this time I have sufficiently proved its adhesive power.

Another problem was the question of space. This enterprise of mine required plenty of room and the studios where I had been painting since my arrival in Vence were not nearly large enough. I therefore immediately arranged to have others built. I needed ample space to spread out on tables, and pin to large boards, all the separate pieces of the preliminary paintings, as well as another place in which first to paint them. The construction of these new studios, begun in December 1955, was to have been completed by the following April, but was not, as a matter of fact, finished until July.

However, I was so anxious to get started on these new works that, in spite of my intention of waiting for my new quarters, I began a whole series of preliminary paintings to be used in these assemblages. After finishing about fifty of them, I could not resist the temptation of taking the scissors and beginning my experiments. Immediately I became so fascinated that, by the time I took possession of my new work rooms, more than forty were completed (I decided to call them Tableaux d'Assemblages), all done in various makeshift studios.

As soon as I began the cutting up of these canvases, I felt that in this method I was going to find what I had looked for in vain from other methods, very nearly the same effects as those obtained in the butterfly-wing collages. Very similar too were the series of colors in these new paintings, in which color was diffused in the same way over the whole picture, so that the exact color was forgotten, eluded analysis, producing a bright pearly shimmering, but by means of what colors it was impossible to say. I had already noticed while making the tiny assemblages of wings, in which so many different colors produced an over-all effect of a diaphanous iridescent haze, impossible to analyze and richly luminous, that here I had found a system of using color diametrically opposed to the decorative use of large areas of strongly contrasting brilliant colors, adopted by painters for the last sixty years—a very much subtler system, in which color was not intended just to strike the eye but, on the contrary, was used in such a way that it could scarcely be recognized. This is very much the way the eye usually perceives real things, landscapes or objects, so that in most cases in trying to reproduce them one would not know what colors to use, the model seeming to be made up of an infinite complexity of shades, impossible to analyze. By this totally different use of color, taking from it all decorative property and aiming only at obtaining an effect that would be striking simply because of the feeling it gives of intense life, I was opening up, it seems to me, a vast new field of research. It was in this direction (keeping constantly in mind the butterfly-wing collages) that the Tableaux d'Assemblages were oriented from the beginning, and have continued to be ever since.

When I stop to consider my idea of using color in shimmerings, with the make-up of the color impossible to discern, my aim being to give the effect of a lively scintillation, it occurs to me that this corresponds to a need of the same order as that which formerly, in many of my drawings and in many of my paintings, made me organize lines and spots so that the objects represented would interfuse with everything around them, resulting in a kind of continuous universal soup with the savor of life itself. Perhaps I was now going to succeed, thanks to my new technique, in getting all the colors to circulate similarly over the whole painting, quickening every part of it with a lustrous quivering, generator of life.

In addition, this new assemblage method, from the very beginning, seemed to lend itself perfectly to the treatment of those subjects which had preoccupied me for months past, being as you know, the grasses and tiny plants growing along the roadside, the roads themselves, and the foot of walls, then the gardens, and soil rich in humus, covered with twigs and decayed leaves with their very complex textures, and finally stony mountain soil overgrown with a small modest vegetation—wild thyme, moss and lichens—carpets of coarse turf (often a demi-synthesis and ambiguity between the themes). Now my Tableaux d'Assemblages had these same themes as their subjects.

Whatever the relative success of these Tableaux d'Assemblages looked at from the point of view of realization, I can say with complete assurance that for anyone who might consider this method as at least a factor of improvisation and experimentation, as a spur to imagination, as a gymnastic exercise to free painting from inherited conventions and inhibiting prejudices, as a stimulant to inventiveness in every domain (subjects, composition, drawing, coloring) or at least as a preliminary means toward the realization of future paintings that would not even resort to this method—it is extremely exciting and fruitful. I feel quite sure at the moment of writing these lines that after a whole year given up to these exercises, whatever paintings I may

Layer of Debris at the Foot of a Wall. 1957. Oil on canvas (assemblage), 8′ 8$^{1}/_{4}$ × 45$^{1}/_{2}$″. Private collection

choose to paint from now on will be strongly marked by this technique, even if they never make use of it. In any case I shall undoubtedly return to it periodically as a source of stimulation and renewal.

An exhibition of these Tableaux d'Assemblages, consisting of 35 items done in Vence between November and December 1956 was held in May 1957 at the Galerie Rive Droite in Paris.

TROISIEME SERIE D'ASSEMBLAGES D'EMPREINTES (*Third Series of Imprint Assemblages*). *Paris, December 1956 to March 1957*

After spending two consecutive years in Vence, almost never leaving it, I returned in December 1956 to my house in Paris for the winter, as by that time my wife had regained her health. During my stay there which lasted until the beginning of April 1957, I undertook a new series of assemblages of imprints in India ink. They were benefited by having been done in a more spacious studio than the one in which I had made the same kind of works in Vence. The pictures show the effect of the greater ease afforded me in the manipulations, and thus, I believe, gained in freedom and boldness. It also seems to me that they owe a good deal to the paintings in a similar technique I had just finished and, in fact, are derived from them. The same themes I have mentioned, either bare ground, or earth embellished with tiny plants and stones, reappear with insistence.

All of them, I think, are dependent on the mental material brought back from Vence, to which my stay in Paris, being far too brief, added nothing. I have already mentioned certain traits of these new assemblages that differed from the earlier ones, and notably that they are much closer to the specific character of imprints from which they stem. On this special character of imprints and its poetic quality, as well as on the technique I employed in those previous imprints, I wrote at length in an article in the April number of *Lettres Nouvelles* [bibl. 35].

In concluding this account, I feel that I must make a confession. Although I am convinced that all these works, which are successively connected with this confession, abound in many very pregnant directive ideas, or at least are susceptible of becoming so and of leading to various very interesting lines of procedure, I am nevertheless conscious of their imperfect

Obscure Stage at the Foot of a Wall. 1957.
India ink (imprint assemblage), 51¹/₂ × 26".
Collection Mr. and Mrs. Samuel M. Kootz,
New York

character in most cases, perhaps in all cases without exception, due to my want of manual dexterity, and to having given too little time to elucidating each one in order to arrive at more completely convincing works (impatient as I always am to go on to new fields of research). I am conscious, as I said, of their unsatisfactory character, especially for anyone who, not knowing as I do the intentions and changes of mood that went into these paintings, quite legitimately demands that they be clear at first glance without the need of commentaries. It is because I am conscious of not having succeeded in doing this, except in very rare cases, that I have thought it necessary to write this memoir.

LIEUX CURSIFS *(Cursive Places). Notes on the twenty-four pictures painted in Vence between April 1 and August 31, 1957*

The twenty-four pictures painted in Vence between the first of April and the thirty-first of August 1957 are closely related to each other, and represent landscapes with fields, paths, houses and people, all sketchily drawn. They are very much like the series of pictures I painted in 1949 called Paysages Grotesques. The personages and other elements suggested in them are drawn with very hasty strokes, even precipitate and uncontrolled, corresponding to the vague idea, which has haunted me for a great many years, that such an excessively rapid way of drawing, brutal even, and without the least care, eliminating as it does all affectations and mannerisms, might bring into being a sort of innocent and primordial figuration that would be most efficacious. For a very long time I have been attracted by the idea of composing large finished pictures using only the most inadequate means, the way people draw who have had no training at all, like the careless scribblings on barracks walls—seeking an equivalent way of painting, just as rude, just as free from the methods of professional artists. I feel that the elements thus depicted acquire, or at least might acquire, because of being drawn in this negligent manner, a much greater dynamic power. I feel that this hasty and very sketchy character of their delineation gives them an effective and tragic shock value—at least as it affects me. In these paintings I have experimented with this mechanism in various ways: sometimes by means of lines carved in the paste with the round end of a spatula, sometimes using rather unattractive heavy black lines painted with a large brush, sometimes, on the contrary, by lines so lightly traced that one can hardly make out the object delineated. Often I took pleasure in maintaining a doubt as to whether the designs were the result of accidents occurring in the paste, due to the impetuous and rather inattentive way of painting, or of my deliberately traced lines. The latter were, in fact, dependent on the accidents, that is to say, they followed the same movement by means of which, it seemed to me, I could get the effect of the whole painting throbbing with the same pulse-beat, lending it great vivacity and endowing it strongly with life. As for the colors employed, I constantly followed my principle of preventing them—like the lines—from being too deliberate, too appropriate. I wanted them to have the same arbitrary, very hasty character, equivocal and indefinite. I did my utmost to make them, as well as the manner of their distribution and application, obey the same mechanisms as the lines. Here are involved certain little problems, which it will be interesting to solve. I would sometimes have recourse to rather brilliant colors (though often engulfing them later with dull tones), sometimes, on the contrary, I would use weak colors, never worrying as to whether or not they were appropriate for the subjects portrayed. In the matter of the lines, as well as the colors, and also the way the paste was applied, in short about everything that went into the make-up of the painting—composition, orientation, etc., I feel that by constantly exploiting the inadaptability of the methods employed, the result of the excessively hasty and arbitrary and paltry character of these methods, and by the *divergence* between what one wished to convey (the places one intended to suggest) and what the hand has traced, it would be possible to give the painting a kind of articulation that might prove most fruitful: a subtle play of ambiguities that would make it easy to vivify the painting with all sorts of changing humors, prevent it from opening on a dead end, keep it open on all sides.

I am convinced that by defining too explicitly the objects and places one intends to evoke, instead of augmenting, one diminishes the intensity of their apparition. It is because a painting without any blanks to be filled, without demanding any effort, no longer acts as a stimulus to the imagination, so that the imagination failing to react, does not kindle sparks in the mind. It is the blanks in a painting that are important, that constitute its power. Moreover, the principle of the matrix governs our perception of all things, and whoever delivers them from the matrix, thus isolating them, takes away three quarters of their virtue. Objects, when our eyes fall upon them, habitually appear to be enveloped, and are an inextricable part of the blurred surround-

Blotting Out Memories. 1957. Oil on canvas, 35 × 46″. Collection Mr. and Mrs. David E. Bright, Beverly Hills

ings we ignore. It is important for the painter who wants to give life to his presentations that he should reconstitute this environment which will bathe all the objects evoked in a life-giving atmosphere. It is this fundamental bath that the painter is called upon to create. After that, everything he chooses to inscribe in the painting, however summarily, will come alive with great force.

In this series of paintings the theme of the *house* constantly recurs. It often has the appearance of a ship, or a wagon tightly closed and impermeable, sometimes with a face at the window. The entrance door is treated with special emphasis and the inhabitant of the house is shown putting his key in the lock.

TOPOGRAPHIES, TEXTUROLOGIES ET QUELQUES PEINTURES. *Notes on the paintings done between September 1 and December 31, 1957*

The exceptionally large number of paintings done in Vence during the last four months of 1957 may be divided into various categories, which I will examine one by one.

I shall first mention a few pictures painted in September which really belong to the series done in previous months, depicting vague landscapes with fields, paths, houses and people.

Except for these few paintings all my works of this period belong to my project for the execution of a cycle of large paintings celebrating the ground. I must begin by saying that it was not carried out to its final conclusion but was confined to preliminary essays, often diverted from their original destination.

My idea was to obtain large paintings by means of assemblages. To that end the first step was collecting a considerable number of basic paintings depicting the different elements that compose the surface of the ground, and out of them later cutting pieces and juxtaposing them in various ways.

What I had in mind was to portray these surfaces without using lines or forms. I meant to evoke any area of bare ground—preferably esplanade or roadway—seen from above, that is, a fragment of a continuous unit, perhaps vaguely divided into zones, just as the ground of a roadway appears when looked at attentively, or when inspiration or one's own discrimination takes over and justifies the transfiguration. I did not, in fact, exclude intervention in depicting these indefinite pieces of ground (in spite of so intractable a subject—or perhaps on that very account) or the part that freedom and the painter's inventiveness might give to circumscribed and well-defined objects, which remain, however cavalierly treated, easily recognizable. What captivated me in the first place was the opportunity afforded of composing paintings by the simple method of juxtaposing textures on which there were no objects with clearly defined contours, and which gave one the same impression as looking down at a vast expanse of ground that could be endlessly prolonged. I decided to call these paintings Topographies.

During this whole period I again experimented assiduously with a method I had already used extensively in the preliminary paintings for my Tableaux d'Assemblages—and even before that in 1955 for Personnages Monolithes. It consists in applying sheets of paper to fresh paint. But, while till now I had always used sheets of newspaper (the marks of the perpendicular folds played a part in the effects obtained), this time, after experimenting with large pieces of various materials, oilcloth, satinette etc., I tried sheets of white drawing paper, first of quite ordinary quality, then pure rag Arches. Often an arresting image would appear on the sheet of paper. I undertook to preserve the ones that interested me. Soon I began working with a view to obtaining imprints rather than to preserving the painting itself. Certain sheets of paper were used for several successive imprints, then I would make duplicates on other sheets. Later, cutting up these papers and assembling the pieces, I made assemblages of oil paintings on paper— afterwards gluing and remounting them. At the same time, I continued my paintings on canvas.

These works on paper, like those on canvas, were directed toward the realization of Topographies. The ones on paper, however, came nearer to what I had in mind than those on canvas. Besides, in the case of the paintings on canvas, my plan suffered from the fact that the elements I had intended to use later on in my assemblages were the ones I put aside, thinking they constituted works engaging enough in themselves to be kept intact, or, in the case of others, their goal had been completely altered by some tempting interpolation which, without modifying anything essential, turned these textures of ground into personages, tables, doors, etc. The result was that in the end there was not enough of the paintings left for my assemblage experiments, so that, of the many Topographies I had in view, only one was completed, which I called *The Little Couch-Grass*, and of a very modest dimension at that. Needless to say I intend to take up this abortive enterprise once more in the near future.

129

Bare Table. 1957. Oil on canvas, 38¹/₄ × 51¹/₄″. World House Galleries, New York

The Withdrawal. 1957. Oil on canvas, 45⅝×35″. Owned by the artist

Again and again these paintings became transformed into Tables. It should be remarked that a table is in a way an elevated piece of ground. It is, moreover, one of the objects to which a man's life is most intimately linked, and is adapted to serve both as a place and an instrument for intellectual pursuits, exemplified by the use of tables in religious worship, in the practice of magic, and in spiritualistic seances. Formerly, in painting tables, I had used the same technique as in Sols et Terrains (1951–52) and then in Pâtes Battues (1953). I might mention in passing that it is always when I am preoccupied by the subject of the ground that the theme of the table crops up.

As I worked on these new tables, I was pleased to feel the awakening of the same enthusiasm, of a very special kind, which this rather odd subject had afforded me in those earlier years, and to find that I could obtain just as convincing effects by means of entirely different techniques. Similarly, in certain paintings depicting either scenes or personages, it pleased me to bring my new techniques to bear on the same kind of themes as those that figured in works as far back as 1943–44. In the course of my work, I have noticed that it is often after a long while, after periods of absence, that one fine day, thanks to all the detours, and by entirely different paths, I stumble upon what I once sought and failed to find.

Among my projects of the last three years was the painting of doors. During my walks in and around Vence, to provide myself with documents, I had made sketches of the various doors I came across, and two years before that, I had even bought a large dilapidated peasant door so that I could study it at leisure in my home. But, since I had no very definite idea of how this subject might be used so as to constitute a painting, I had till now done nothing with all this material. One of the paintings intended, like the others, as an element of the ground in my Topographies, seemed to lend itself, with only a few supplementary touches, to such a trans-formation into a door, completely filling as it did the entire rectangle of the painting. A little while later I decided to cut up this rectangle, attach it to a board and pin up around it various other elements previously taken from other paintings to represent a wall, a doorstep, and the ground. Certain of these elements, intended for my assemblages, were the result of a special technique. It consisted in shaking a brush over the painting spread out on the floor, covering it with a spray of tiny droplets. This is the technique, known as "Tyrolean," that masons use in plastering walls to obtain certain mellowing effects. But, instead of brushes, they use little

opposite: *Door with Couch-Grass*. 1957. Oil on canvas (assemblage), $74^{3}/_{8} \times 57^{1}/_{2}$″. The Solomon R. Guggenheim Museum, New York

133

Mirandoliana. 1957. Oil on canvas (assemblage), 36¹/₄ × 53″. Collection Ayala and Sam Zacks, Toronto

The Voice of the Soil. 1957. Oil on canvas, $44^{1}/_{2} \times 57^{1}/_{2}$". World House Galleries, New York

branches of trees—juniper, box, etc.—and they have different ways of shaking them to get the particular effect they want. I combined this technique with others—successive layers, application of sheets of paper, scattering sand over the painting, scratching it with the tines of a fork. In this way I produced finely worked sheets that gave the impression of teeming matter, alive and sparkling, which I could use to represent a piece of ground, but which could also evoke all kinds of indeterminate textures, and even galaxies and nebulae. But most of these paintings, about fifteen in number, which I called Texturologies, I also decided to keep intact, instead of cutting them up for my assemblages.

I must mention in particular the painting entitled *Terres théâtrales* (plum, gold and sulfur) because it illustrates certain psychological phenomena which intermittently manifest themselves in me. It is a question of reverting to a style similar to the one I was aiming at in the pictures of 1942–44, a style that, for lack of a better word, I call "theatrical." The idea is to represent things by boldly simplified, exaggerated and even burlesque means, the coloring brutal, the outlines excessively marked, the lines black and very conspicuous. I even prefer objects that are the least suited to this treatment, as in the painting referred to, which portrays only an ill-defined terrain, possibly vague fields. The pictures of this kind, unlike my other paintings, instead of merging all the elements in a sort of continuum, in a bottomless bath that shows they belong to unknown and more or less dangerous realms—at least completely foreign to the spheres where men abide—introduce a diversity and an expressive motility where reality shows only uniformity, and has but little interest. I think I might say that these paintings aim at showing human emotion, man's particular ways (innocent like the ways of children when they draw) of transcribing the sights spread out before his eyes and the complete harmony of man's nature, his life, and his condition with these sights, but also the painter's very positive *intervention* (it being always understood that I expect, nevertheless, that finally this excess of easy detachment with which he has treated the objects will give anyone looking at the painting a vague impression of an alarming error). In short, the paintings in this vein rest on lively *humanization* of the subjects treated—and this is what makes me think of the theater or of circus clowns—while, on the contrary many of my other paintings, I believe, rest on the *dehumanization* of the subjects, on a kind of de-individualization both of the subjects and of the painter himself. I realize that two different and contrary claims keep me swinging between the

opposite: *Person Attached to the Soil.* 1958. Oil on canvas (assemblage), 58 × 44½". Collection Mr. and Mrs. Arnold H. Maremont, Chicago

attraction of two opposite poles according to the moment, and often result in paintings that have something of each. To the humanizing and interventionist humor evidently belong the grotesque Vaches, 1954, while the Texturologies are consecrated to the dehumanizing or, as one might say, metaphysical or Lamaistic humor.

In the same way, on the technical side, I always feel that I am balancing between two opposite extremes which will be readily seen in my paintings. At one extreme there is the use of very boldly drawn lines, either black strokes or incisions in the paste, while at the other the aim, on the contrary, is to obtain pure painting effects, in which only the inner textures function, and from which all external lines and forms are excluded. I have long been pursued by the idea of at last liberating painting from design, of giving pure painting every chance, with the painted surfaces its only language.

Translated by Louise Varèse

Jean Dubuffet: The Recent Work – *by Peter Selz*

Dubuffet continued painting Texturologies until 1959; indeed, the Beards that were to follow are texturologies of a particular kind, while the Materiologies of 1960 are also closely related to them in spirit. The Texturologies are free terrestial surfaces. The artist here avoids all figurative subject matter, anecdote, narrative. Yet, unlike most painters of his generation, he does not paint abstractions. The Texturologies are descriptive—not narrative—views of the ground, seen from above.

Again and again in his *Memoir* Dubuffet emphasizes his opposition to the careful analysis of an object, maintaining that it is against man's nature to stare at things and to make inventories of their parts. Dubuffet is always conscious of the quick glance which takes in a great deal more than a particular point of focus because it is aware of a world infinitely greater than the specific fragment, a world expanding around us on all sides. He recognizes the organic, internal mobility of nature, whose essence was discovered—in a very different and more sensuous way—by the old Monet in his water landscapes. In the Texturologies Dubuffet paints blurred peripheral areas that are usually ignored, though they are perceived unconsciously. By an inspired observation of specific surfaces of matter, he actually delves beyond conscious perception of a fragmentary world toward an apprehension of the unbroken phenomena of continuity. The Texturologies reject any center of interest or other compositional devices. There are no objects with precise contours or shapes, no lines and no limits except the frame. Instead of form he has provided us with formlessness. By painting surfaces which are both continuous and endless, he evokes a vision of infinity.[31] "These pictures provide me with peace," he writes, "... great peace of rugs and naked and empty plains, silently uninterrupted distances whose homogeneity and continuity cannot be altered. I love homogeneous worlds with neither landmarks nor boundaries, which are like the sea, snowy mountains, deserts and steppes."[32]

The Texturologies and that gigantic series of lithographs, *Les Phénomenes*—begun in 1958 and amounting to 324 prints—deal with earth and wall surfaces, both of which have always

Texturology X: Rose Marbleized. 1957. Oil on canvas, 44⁷/₈ × 51³/₈". Private collection

The Example Set by the Soil. 1958. Oil on canvas, 50³/₄ × 63³/₄″. Owned by the artist

Soothsayer. 1958. Oil on canvas, 45³/₄×35″. Galerie Europe, Paris

142

The Sententious One. 1958. Oil on canvas, 36¹/₄×30″.
Collection Mr. and Mrs. Elias M. Pinto, New York

The Heights of Marriage (Portraits of Werner and Nora Schenk). 1958. Oil on canvas, 36¹/₄×28³/₄″.
Private collection

captivated Dubuffet. They describe land and sea, the vapors of the atmosphere, the sky with its milky way and galaxies.

Dubuffet has always felt that a painting—like a child—has a right to a name, and the nomenclature of the Texturologies is especially inspired. The titles include: *Le Manteau de terre (The Cloak of Earth), Langage des caves (The Voice of the Caves), Lit de silence (The Bed of Silence), La Physique du sol (The Nature of the Earth),* etc. Only Klee's titles—though they are more whimsical—were similarly inventive and had a comparable poetic ring.

Of earlier painters in this century, only Klee, Picasso and Ernst manifest a similar versatility.

In the summer of 1921 Picasso painted pictures as diverse as the cubist *Three Musicians* and the classical *Three Women at the Spring*. During 1958 and 1959, while engaged on the Texturologies, Dubuffet turned again to the human figure, this time to the mock-heroic Figures-Augures (Soothsayers). Instead of the all-over, undifferentiated diffusion of the Texturologies, these are concentrated, axial figure compositions of urgent power whose antecedents appear in such canvases as *Artful Hubbub* (page 115) from the Monolithic Personages series of the summer of 1955.

The canvas called *Soothsayer* of May 1958 is a frightening image which looks like the large, gnarled bole of a tree, from which emerge unmistakably human features: eyes, faint suggestions of nose, mouth and hands. It resembles some primordial creature, faintly recalling certain carvings from the Sepic River as well as the Hamadryads of Greek mythology who, it was thought, formed an integral part of the trees they guarded.

The Sentencious One of the same period is not a nature spirit but rather an intellectual ghost, even under his shroud. This blue-eyed phantom, with his moldy body, is quite a sophisticated fellow, though hamstrung by the proprieties. *The Attentive One* is a much more human and frightened ghost, whose face and body have been created by fluid, calligraphic shapes.

In October 1958, Dubuffet painted *The Heights of Marriage*, a double-portrait of his friends Werner and Nora Schenk, which might be called a stele to connubial bliss. Stolid and stable, they take themselves very seriously in this satire on the bourgeois couple.

The Figures Fantomatiques (Phantom Figures), a small series made in the autumn of 1959, develop from the Figures-Augures. *The Black Eye* of November 1959 has an even more spectral appearance than the earlier ghosts. This one seems to materialize accidentally out of flowing paint and running stains. In spite of his soft outlines and vague features, this is a haunting image, as memorable as the Cheshire Cat (page 146).

At the same time as Dubuffet was making the Phantom Figures, he began working on his great series of Beards. He first turned to the theme of the beard in May 1959 by means of Assemblages d'Empreintes in India ink, which developed from the Texturology drawings. In the autumn of that year the large, thinly painted oils of the Beards were created. The whole series was exhibited as a unit at the Galerie Daniel Cordier in Paris in April 1960 in an exhibition called *As-tu cueilli la fleur de barbe?*.

The Attentive One. 1958. Oil on canvas, 37 × 29¹/₄″. Private collection

Black Eye. 1959. Oil on canvas, 45×35″. Private collection

Beard of Uncertain Returns. 1959. Oil on canvas, 45³/₄×35¹/₈″. The Museum of Modern Art, New York. Mrs. Sam A. Lewisohn Fund

147

Beard Map. 1959. Oil on canvas, 51³/₄×38¹/₂". Collection Mr. and Mrs. Edward J. Mathews, New York

Deriving from the Texturologies, the Beards have the surfaces of large agglomerated and distending masses. In shape, they often suggest the earlier Tables, but here Texturology and Table have again become anthropomorphic, with everything relating to man. The surfaces no longer expand into infinity but are clearly focused into a frontal image like the Soothsayers, although they have become even more monumental in their stance.

Some of the Beards, such as *the Beard of Uncertain Returns*, look like gravel runs and have that geological feeling inherent in so much of Dubuffet's work. Some resemble great rock formations or age-old boulders predating man's presence on this planet. Or they appear to be survivors of ancient barbaric—that is to say, bearded—civilizations. Their shapes recall the menhirs of Stonehenge and the Winged Bulls from Assyrian palaces. The beard is the age-less symbol of manhood, and most cultures worshiped bearded divinities such as the Greek earth gods, Titans and Cyclops as well as the Olympians who followed them, the vengeful Hebraic god as well as the first person of the Trinity. It is the memory of these archetypes that Dubuffet now evokes. In a letter to this author, written at the very time that he began working on the Beards, he says: "I have liked to carry the human image onto a plane of seriousness where the futile embellishments of esthetics have no longer any place, onto a plane of high ceremony, of solemn office of celebration by helping myself with what Joseph Conrad calls: 'a mixture of familiarity and terror,' out of which the devotion is made which many religious minds offer to their gods and which does not, at times, exclude the use of swear words directed at them."[33]

The beard has become the essence. The whole world of geology and mythology—i. e. earth and man—seems to be contained in the great and majestic beard of the *Beard Map*. These immense surfaces are shields, aprons, cover-alls. They are magic screens, almost absolute in their scale. At times man's face is limited only to a bare indication of eyes and mouth. He clutches it in *Beard Offering* or holds it up like a great vessel in *Beard Vase*. Man is reduced to being a beard carrier; or is he *elevated* to this position since the beards have indeed become a universe?

> *Ta barbe est mon bateau*
> *Ta barbe est mon eau j'y navigue*
> *Barbe de flux et d'influx*
> *Bain de barbe et pluie de barbe*
> *Elément tissé de fluides*
> *Tapisserie de récits*
> *De la barbe du birbe.*[34]

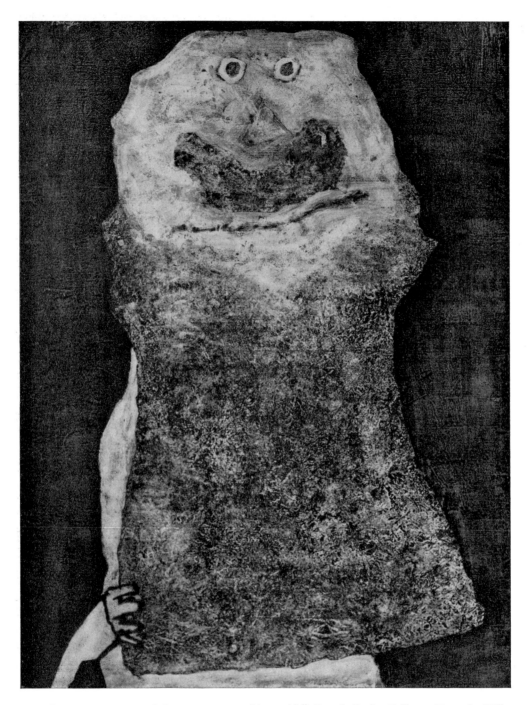

Beard Offering. 1959. Oil on canvas, 51^1/$_8$×38^1/$_4$″. Frank Perls Gallery, Beverly Hills

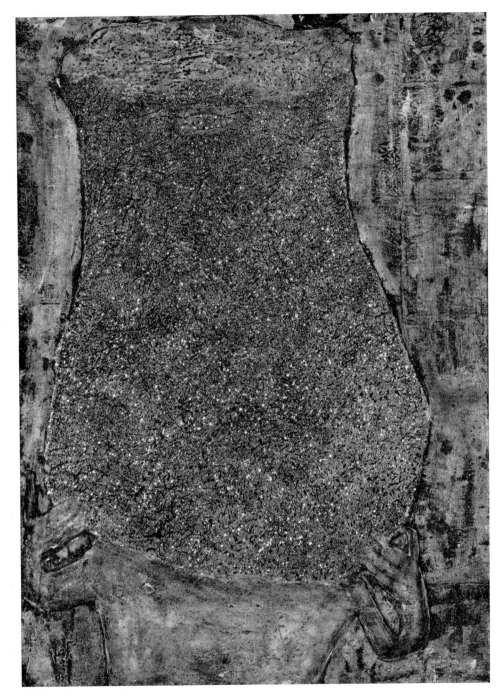

Beard Vase. 1959. Oil on canvas, 51¹/₄ × 38¹/₄". Galerie E. Beyeler, Basel

The Sea of Skin. 1959. Botanic elements: century plant leaves, $21^3/4 \times 18''$. Owned by the artist

The Forest. 1959. Botanic elements: leaves, $20^1/2 \times 22^1/2''$. Private collection

Dubuffet is constantly in need of altering his material and technique as he changes his subject matter. The new materials and techniques, in fact, furnish him with the reasons for new exploration while simultaneously leading him toward further discovery as they tap ever new resources of his imagination. The substances concocted, the tools used, are all of extreme importance: he employs them consciously to accumulate a series of obstacles which must be overcome in order for the semi-arbitrary imagery to evolve. This is to keep the spectator from easy recognition so that the final enjoyment and wonder of unexpected revelation will be greatly augmented by the epiphanic shock of sudden awareness.

In August 1959, even prior to the great paintings of the Beards, he began to explore vegetal substances, which he would mount directly on wooden panels. He used leaves of agave and

The Gardener. 1959. Botanic elements: leaves, 26¹/₂ × 20″. Collection Mr. and Mrs. Arnold H. Maremont, Chicago

artichoke, tobacco, camomile and the Medlar tree, banana peels and orange rinds, calyxes of flowers and fragments of various ferns, herbs, shrubs, trees, vines, flowers and fruits—forming a kind of mosaic never seen before. Dubuffet was occupied with these Eléments Botaniques (Botanic Elements) until the end of the year and showed forty of them—all small in scale—in a distinctive exhibition at Arthur Tooth and Sons in London in May 1960.

Although it is true that his forms in the Eléments Botaniques are determined largely by the materials he employs—the leaves, stems, peels and blossoms, it is just as obvious that the end products are results of an *idée fixe* which runs throughout his work. Both things seem to be equally true. That is, he pastes down the leaves in such a way that, although they form a landscape, their textures and patterns are sharply revealed and call attention to their specific structure. Moreover, they closely resemble his painted landscapes with their high horizons or over-all expanse, or they look like his "tables" or his "stones" in their rough, monotonous surfaces. Similarly, his Arcimboldesque leaf-men and leaf-heads are stiff, frontal figures with

Bearded Head. 1959. Driftwood. 11¹/₂″ high. World House Galleries, New York

The Old Man of the Beach. 1959. Driftwood, 13³/₈″ high. Collection D.B.C.

The Scornful One. 1959. Driftwood, 16¹/₂″ high. Collection D.B.C.

grotesque eyes and mouths and straight, awkward arms and legs. In other words, they grow from essentially the same frontal concept as do the Portraits, the Corps de Dames, the Beards. Yet it seems true that he will paste down an element first, a leaf or a flower, and then see in it that essential image which he wishes to work out upon the surface. One may say that Dubuffet starts with tangible nature itself and then transmutes it by means of his mind and hands, arriving at a new, personal and unique image of that very nature.

The Blind One. 1959. Metal foil, 12⅝″ high. Owned by the artist

Sometimes little transmutation seems necessary when nature has already provided it. Extending the Eléments Botaniques into three dimensions, he created a series of successors to the Little Statues of Precarious Life of 1954. They relate most closely to a figure like the *Magician* (page 91) where slag and roots become an object of ritual which might turn up on the altar of a stag-worshipping cult. Gathering driftwood from the Mediterranean beaches after storms in the autumn of 1959, he found his astonishing figurations among the flotsam. Perhaps art has always imitated nature; perhaps man has always seen the world through the form-giving eyes of artists. We are reminded of the lady who told Whistler at a dinner party that she had just crossed Battersea Bridge and found that London looked like one of his nocturnes, to which Whistler ironically replied: "Thank you ma'am, nature's improving." So Dubuffet, coming upon objects which looked like imitations of his work, mounted these apparitions from the sea. Sometimes he would help them along to create fully *his* image or he would leave them as they were discovered.

Oberon. 1960. Papier mâché, 35″ high.
Owned by the artist

The small driftwood *Bearded Head* of December 1959, looks, indeed, like one of Dubuffet's Beards. This gnarled, warted fellow with his deep-set eyes, squashed nose and cruel expression might almost be a late classical image of the Barbarian. Sometimes these figures are grotesquely weathered and shriveled like *The Old Man of the Beach*, or they are in a state of metamorphosis between animal and vegetal form like *The Scornful One*—a poetic little personage whose classical *contraposto* stance contrasts amusingly with the grass growing from the top of his head.

Crumbling up silver foil and often blackening it he gives his objects all the associations of *pompes funèbres*. *The Blind One* is a small head with the defenseless, vulnerable look which the blind so often have because, unable to watch others, they have never learned to form those social masks we carry about with us. This is a remarkable little statue which has the essentially haptic form—emphasizing touch impressions and muscular sensations—used by the blind in their own art expressions.

Several of the sculptures done between the autumn of 1959 and 1960 were made of reinforced papier mâché, often colored with inks and oil paints. In the more recent work, like *Oberon* of June 1960, they have attained a super-life-size which reinforces their appearance of unbridled primitive power.

The luminous, crumpled silver foil of some of the statues appears again in the Matériologies —objects somewhere on the border between bas-reliefs and painting. Thick pulverizations of papier mâché as well as crushed and warped silver foil are applied onto masonite panels. In certain of the pictures, Dubuffet applied the papier mâché over a plastic paste; sometimes he used vinyl paste and polyester resins as well as sand and fragments of mica (page 159).

The substance is even thicker than in the Hautes Pâtes of the late forties or the Landscapes of the early fifties. Now the geologist with his magnifying glass has plunged even more deeply into the earth in his attempt to wrest secrets from stone, mud and clay. Dubuffet has always felt that a crystal was as alive as a leaf or a bird and now he gives substance to matter itself, matter which evolves slowly but has not achieved a definite form and will always stay undefined. Its nature does not lend itself to static interpretation. Again there is no central composition, no focus, no form in the traditional sense. As we contemplate these dense surfaces, they seem to become removed, distant. Solidity turns into a void. If the Texturologies evoke memories of wind and sand, the Matériologies imply soil and rock. This is a much heavier world

Life without Man III. 1960. Papier mâché and plastic paste on composition board, 25$^1/_2 \times$ 32″. Collection Jean Planque, Paris

and its flow is slower. We see fragments of the universe as if looking at the pitted surfaces of stars by means of huge reflecting telescopes or at the porous texture of sedimentary rocks observed through the electron microscope. In the Matériologies, where he seems most abstract, Dubuffet also becomes most metaphysical. He carefully and deliberately recreates a visual image of nature's own aimless purpose, not with the intent of revealing knowledge but with the hope of achieving understanding. In 1957 he wrote: "Socrates, the point is not to know oneself, but to forget."[35]

In Dubuffet's development as an artist a systolic period of concentration is often followed by its obverse: the diastole of expansion and enlargement. So the careful observation of the surfaces of matter gives way, in 1961, to broad panoramic views of city life. Instead of an involvement with the textures of nature, the artist now turns to social commentary. He portrays his fellow humans eating in cavernous restaurants, walking in the streets with purposeless hurry, displaying themselves in department stores, driving in octopus-shaped little Fords and Citroëns with the compulsive anxiety of trapped animals.

These recent, brightly painted city scenes resemble the views of Paris and subway pictures of the early forties although texture, space and deployment of figures have become much more complex. These people, generally without arms, are presented either in a schematic front view or in a conspicuous profile. The only other place where these profiles, with their huge frontal eyes, their prominent noses and quickly receding skulls, appear is in the Sumerian narrative reliefs dating from the fourth and early third millenium. But now these figures move in fantastic relationships to one another. Some are upright; others are on their side or upside down and piled on each other without clear spatial structure of any sort.

The result is a jumbled panorama effect of the city in which people, cars, lettering, all make up a wild flat pattern—not unlike a crazy quilt or a jig-saw puzzle. The inscriptions, drawn from and satirizing the signs on shop fronts, consist of plays on words and are used for both associative and formal reasons. In their relationship to the figures, they recall the early woodcuts in fifteenth-century block-books in which pictures and didactic text are combined in a single print, a tradition which continues in popular imagery into the twentieth century with the comic strip. Dubuffet's new cityscapes seem to trace man's voyage through modern life from L'Estomaque to Désastres (page 161).

Business Prospers. 1961. Oil on canvas, 65 × 86⅝". Owned by the artist

The Automobile, Flower of Industry. 1961. Oil on canvas, 86×65″. Owned by the artist

The fluctuations in Dubuffet's style from period to period comprise a rare phenomenon in the history of painting. Yet, in spite of what appear to be extreme contrasts in subject matter and medium, there is an underlying consistency to his work. In both the Matériologies and the recent city scenes, he continues to establish disparaged values. Important as it is, however, this commitment to ignoble types of subject matter is only one factor of the unity which can be discerned in his work. The seemingly abstract landscapes of the early fifties are, as we have seen, easily transposed into tables or stones, and their surfaces and conceptual realizations resemble the Corps de Dames. Many of the landscapes hardly differentiate between man and objects; divisions are purposely blurred. Dubuffet attempts to break man's isolation from matter, to place him in a continuous whole. Similarly the Texturologies derive from an apprehension of sand and earth, of road surfaces and "vast sidereal cosmogonies" re-appearing in the textures of human beards. The sculptured heads of 1960 with their black funereal sheen are closely related to the Matériologies.

The pervading unity in his work is thus one final result of Dubuffet's amalgamation of apparent opposites. When he makes up a painting from "a few fragments of a homogeneous universe," he is both purposeful and rational in permitting, indeed, in stimulating the action of the irrational elements of accident and chance. Opposed to the cold rationality of the intellect, he still sees clearly that "art addresses itself to the mind"[36] of man.

Dubuffet, then, attempts to bridge the gap between mind and emotion in art. His feeling for continuous organic rhythms which penetrate all aspects of nature relates his work to the Romantic tradition with its pantheist concepts and its "sense and taste for the infinite."[37] But Dubuffet's avowal of pantheist unity is much more tangible and concrete than that of the Romanticists, for it is expressed primarily by means of the material itself. There appears in Dubuffet's work a new fusion of form, content and material—beyond the unity of form and content essential to all art.

The Walk. 1961. Oil on canvas, 35 × 45³/₄". Kunstmuseum, Silkeborg, Denmark

Statement on Paintings of 1961 – *by Jean Dubuffet*

The principle thing about [my paintings of this year] is that they are in complete contrast to those of the Texturology and Materiology series that I did previously. They are in every way the opposite. I believe more and more that my paintings of the previous years avoided in subject and execution specific human motivations. To paint the earth the painter tended to become the earth and to cease to be man—that is, to be painter. In reaction against this absenteeist tendency my paintings of this year put into play in all respects a very insistent *intervention*. The presence in them of the painter now is constant, even exaggerated. They are full of personages, and this time their role is played with spirit. It seems to me that in the whole development of my work there is a constant fluctuation between bias for personages and bias against them. Besides I should mention that the imitations, developments and variations which have been made from my paintings of the "materiologic" type by so many painters in these last years have contributed, no doubt, in turning me from this path and sending me in the opposite direction. My Haute Pâtes of 1945 and the following years, then my Sols et Terrains of 1951 and 1952 had at the time an extraordinary and supernatural character which enchanted me. However, they no longer have this power for me, now that one finds in the windows of all the art galleries of the world paintings stemming from the same spiritual positions, and which have more or less borrowed their themes, style, color, and composition. I feel a need that every work of art should in the highest degree lift one out of context, provoking a surprise and a shock. A painting does not work for me if it is not completely unexpected. Hence my new concern, which at least gives me the satisfaction of being taken to territory where no one else has been.[38]

Notes to the Text

1 Hans Prinzhorn, *Bildnerei der Geisteskranken* (The Art of the Insane), Berlin, Julius Springer, 1922. It is worth noting, in connection with Dubuffet's *art brut* collection, that four years after publishing his book on psychotic art, Prinzhorn issued a volume on the art of prisoners: *Bildnerei der Gefangenen*, Berlin, Axel Juncker, 1926.

2 Dubuffet, *Prospectus aux amateurs de tout genre*, Paris, Gallimard, 1946, page 17.

3 Peter Selz, *New Images of Man*, New York, Museum of Modern Art, 1959, page 62.

4 Leonardo da Vinci, Treatise on Painting, pars. 93, 261.

5 Brassai's photographs of the graffiti of Paris date back to 1931 and were published as early as 1933 in *Minotaure*. Over a period of thirty years now he has assembled the most astonishing photographs of wall images which, together with Dubuffet's paintings, opened the door to a whole new world of the imagination. Both Brassai and Dubuffet were stimulated by the powerful imagery of the scratchings made by children on the old walls of narrow alleyways. Brassai comments: "We are worlds away from the sweetness of child-art. All becomes earnest, raw, harsh, barbaric. It is usually an isolated being, a prey to anxious conflicts, whose hand scratches these lines. Childhood is no golden age, but the age of torment. A whole lifetime is sometimes not enough to wear away its scars. These tragic, and even hideous, masks bear witness to the suffering enclosed in the soul of the child." Brassai, "The Art of the Wall," *The Saturday Book*, vol. 18, The Macmillan Company, 1958, page 245.

6 Dubuffet, "Empreintes," *Les Lettres Nouvelles*, No. 48, April 1957, page 508.

7 René Huyghe, "Dubuffet," *Arts*, Paris, May 17, 1946.

8 A few critics were aware of the importance of his pictures almost from the beginning. Georges Limbour began his studies of the artist in 1944. Jean Paulhan wrote the preface to the catalogue of the 1944 show and Michel Tapié a succinct introduction to the 1946 exhibition. Gladys Delmar mentioned his work first in this country in 1945, and Clement Greenberg praised his painting as early as 1946 when he recognized Dubuffet as "the most original painter to have come out of the School of Paris since Miró" (Greenberg, *The Nation*, June 29, 1946, page 793). Henry McBride and Robert Goldwater also acclaimed his work as early as 1947. For other American criticism of the late forties see note 26.

9 Henri Focillon, *The Life of Forms in Art*, New York, Wittenborn, Schultz, 1948, page 39.

10 Dubuffet, "Notes du Peintre — Portraits," in Georges Limbour, *Tableau bon levain à vous de cuire la pâte*, Paris, René Drouin, 1953, page 91. In this note added to Limbour's book, Dubuffet explained the purpose of his portraits.

11 Catalogue, Galerie René Drouin, Paris, October 1947.

12 Pierre Matisse introduced Dubuffet to the United States as early as 1946, first showing him in a group show with Picasso, Rouault, Chagall, Miró. He presented the artist's first important one-man

show here in 1947. The Portraits here discussed were shown in his gallery in 1948.

[13] A comparison between Dubuffet's Dentists and Toulouse-Lautrec's *The Tracheotomy* in the Clark museum in Williamstown, Mass., indicates a similar type of observation and attitude on the part of the two artists. Lautrec's art, after all, also "rehabilitates disparaged values."

[14] Dubuffet, *Prospectus, op. cit.*, page 43.

[15] Dubuffet, *Prospectus, op. cit.*, pages 53–54.

[16] There is, of course, an ambivalence here. His friends are among the intellectual elite of Paris. Dubuffet himself is clearly a sophisticated intellectual, and one wonders whether his desire for the "barbaric" and the "brut" may not be a wish for compensation.

[17] Dubuffet, *L'art brut préferé aux arts culturels*, Paris, Galerie René Drouin, 1949 (no pagination).

[18] Georges Limbour, *Table bon levain, op. cit.*, pages 56–61.

[19] In 1952, the collection, increased to over 1000 objects by more than 200 different persons, was finally sent to Dubuffet's friend, Alfonso Ossorio, a painter whom he esteems highly. It is now housed in Ossorio's studio in East Hampton, Long Island. Dubuffet himself has continued to collect such materials, never ceasing to be intrigued by this estranged and frightening world.

[20] Dubuffet, "Corps de Dames," in Limbour, *Table bon levain, op. cit.*, pages 94–95.

[21] Michel Tapié, "Dubuffet, The Terrible," *Paris News Post*, November 5, 1950.

[22] A fascinating event in the history of modern art is the simultaneous execution of de Kooning's series of *Women* and Dubuffet's *Corps de Dames*. Not only do they appear at the same time, but each series is important in the artist's oeuvre. In addition to similarity in theme—each series strongly attacks the female image—there is also a curious stylistic resemblance, particularly between Dubuffet's drawings of the *Corps de Dames* and de Kooning's paintings—both dated 1950. They arrived at this comparable image from entirely different points of departure: de Kooning, working in New York, carries on the European Cubist tradition. His concepts of space, his structure, even his imagery builds on Picasso's early Cubist compositions as well as the heads of the late thirties. Dubuffet, working in Paris, breaks almost entirely with Western tradition and looks at crude wall scratchings rather than at "art."

[23] Dubuffet, "Corps de Dames," in *op. cit.* page 94.

[24] Dubuffet, *Prospectus, op. cit.*, page 54.

[25] Dubuffet, *Landscaped Tables, Landscapes of the Mind, Stones of Philosophy*. Introduction to catalogue, Pierre Matisse Gallery, New York, 1952.

[26] *Life*, December 20, 1948, page 20: "Dead End Art—A Frenchman's Mud-and-Rubble Paintings Reduce Modernism to a Joke." Here it was suggested: "there is more human dignity in Al Capp's Dogpatch than in the whole of Dubuffet's gaga cosmos." *New York World-Telegram*, Dec. 6, 1948, p. 17: "Dubuffet's Work Is Savagely Aggressive With Lines Like the Scrawl of a Child." Emily Genauer wrote about his "debasing and perverting the very nature of art," which, of course, is what the artist really had in mind, but with a different meaning. The specialized art magazines manifested a similar attitude: *The Art Digest*, December 1948, page 18: "...seldom in the oils is there anything ingratiating enough to compensate for the conscious crudity of the drawing ..."

Art News, February 1950, page 48: "... whether these conscious apings of the work of children have any meaning beyond their exploitation of coarse and unexpected mediums (sic) is, perhaps, a question for the psychiatrist." This was as late as 1950. (For more favorable criticism by Americans like Greenberg, McBride and Goldwater see note 8).

27 This lecture, dedicated to his friend and collector, the late Maurice Culberg, was first distributed in mimeographed form and then published almost in its entirety in the catalogue of his World House exhibition in 1960.

28 The introductory essay for this catalogue, quoted on page 63–72 was written in French and then translated into English by Dubuffet with the aid of his friend Marcel Duchamp.

29 Dubuffet, "Portraits," in Limbour, *Table bon levain, op. cit.*, page 91.

30 Large excerpts from the *Memoir*, unedited by the artist, were originally published in the catalogue of Dubuffet's retrospective exhibition at the Musée des Arts Décoratifs in Paris in 1960 (bibl. 181). They are republished here, but for reasons of space a number of deletions, such as the important notes on his graphic works, had to be made.

31 In this respect, Dubuffet's Texturologies are strongly suggestive of the work of Mark Tobey. But, whereas Tobey's painting derives from a mystical feeling about the universe, Dubuffet's point of departure is specificity and an examination of tangible experiences.

32 Dubuffet, "Texturologies, Topographies," *Les Lettres Nouvelles*, Paris, April 22, 1959, page 10.

33 Dubuffet, in Selz, *op. cit.*, page 62.

34 Dubuffet, from his poem, "*La Fleur de Barbe,*" *Dossiers du Collège de Pataphysique,* Nos. 10 and 11, Paris, page 6.

>Your beard is my boat
>Your beard is the sea on which I sail
>Beard of flux and influx
>Beard-bath and rain of beards
>Element woven of fluids
>Tapestry of tales

35 Dubuffet, "Empreintes," *Les Lettres Nouvelles*, *op. cit.*, page 520.

36 Dubuffet, "Anticultural Positions," World House catalogue.

37 This is how Friedrich Schleiermacher, the leading theologian and philosopher of the Romantic movement, defined religion in his lectures *On Religion* in 1799.

38 Dubuffet, letter to the author, December 21, 1961.

Major Exhibitions

Asterisks indicate known publication of catalogues or checklists for the exhibition.

ONE-MAN SHOWS

1944 PARIS. Galerie René Drouin. Oct. 20–Nov. 18 *

1945 PARIS. Galerie André. Apr. 14–30. (Lithographs) *

1946 PARIS. Galerie René Drouin. May 3–June 1. ("Mirobolus, Macadam & Cie. Hautes Pâtes") *

1947 NEW YORK. Pierre Matisse Gallery. Jan. 7–Feb. 1 *

1947 PARIS. Galerie René Drouin. Oct. 7–31. ("Portraits.") * See bibl. 165

1947 NEW YORK. Pierre Matisse Gallery. Oct. 10–Nov. 1. (Lithographs) *

1948 NEW YORK. Pierre Matisse Gallery. Nov. 30–Dec. 31 *

1949 BRUSSELS. Galerie le Diable par la Queue. Dec. *

1950 NEW YORK. Pierre Matisse Gallery. Jan. *

1950 PARIS. Galerie Nina Dausset. Feb. ("La Métromanie, ou les Dessous de la Capitale, par Jean Paulhan, calligraphié et orné de dessins par Jean Dubuffet")

1951 NEW YORK. Pierre Matisse Gallery. Jan. 9–Feb. 3 *

1951 PARIS. Galerie Rive Gauche. Mar. ("Pour connaître mieux Jean Dubuffet")

1951 CHICAGO. The Arts Club. Dec. 18, 1951– Jan. 23, 1952 *

1952 NEW YORK. Pierre Matisse Gallery. Feb. 12–Mar. 1. ("Landscaped Tables, Landscapes of the Mind, Stones of Philosophy")

1952 PARIS. Société Nationale d'Horticulture de France. Sept. 8–17. ("Sols et Terrains.") Typewritten catalogue in 5 copies only *

1953 PARIS. Galerie La Hune. Dec. (Lithographs and "Terres radieuses" [ink drawings]) *

1954 STOCKHOLM. Galerie Blanche. Jan.–Feb. (Lithographs)

1954 PARIS. Cercle Volney. Mar. 17–Apr. 17. * See bibl. 167

1954 PARIS. Galerie Rive Gauche. Oct. 19–Nov. 10. ("Petites statues de la vie précaire") *

1954 NEW YORK. Pierre Matisse Gallery. Nov. 23–Dec. 31. (Recent paintings, collages and drawings) *

1955 LONDON. Institute of Contemporary Arts. Mar. 29–Apr. 30. * See bibl. 168

1955 VENCE. Galerie Les Mages. Oct. 1–3. *

1956 NEW YORK. Pierre Matisse Gallery. Feb. 21–Mar. 17. (Paintings and Assemblages d'empreintes, 1954–1955.) * See bibl. 170

1956 BEVERLY HILLS, CALIF. Frank Perls Gallery. Apr. 24–May 26 *

1956 PARIS. Galerie Rive Gauche. May 15–June 6. ("Assemblages d'empreintes," 1954–1955) *

1957 PARIS. Galerie Rive Droite. Apr. 30–May 23. ("Tableaux d'assemblages") *

1957 LEVERKUSEN. Städtisches Museum Schloss Morsbroich. Aug. 23–Oct. 13. * See bibl. 171

1958 MILAN. Galleria del Naviglio. Jan. 25–Feb. 14 *

1958 NEW YORK. Pierre Matisse Gallery. Feb. 4–22.

("Peintures d'assemblages, graffiti, sols, tex-turologie" and other recent works done in 1956 and 1957.) * See bibl. 172

1958 LONDON. Arthur Tooth Gallery. Apr. 29–May 23.* See bibl. 173

1958 ROME. Galleria d'Arte Selecta. May 3–30*

1958 FRANKFORT. Galerie Daniel Cordier. Dec. 1958–Jan. 1959. ("Lob der Erde") *

1959 PARIS. Galerie Daniel Cordier. Apr. 28–June 7. ("Célébration du Sol") *

1959 NEW YORK. Pierre Matisse Gallery. Nov. 10–Dec. 12. (Retrospective exhibition 1943–1959.) * See bibl. 175

1960 STOCKHOLM. Galerie Pierre. Opened April 21. (Color lithographs)

1960 PARIS. Galerie Daniel Cordier. Apr. 27–May 31 ("As-tu cueilli la fleur de barbe?") * See bibl. 176

1960 MILAN. Galleria Blu. May

1960 LONDON. Arthur Tooth Gallery. May 31–June 18. ("Eléments botaniques.") * See bibl. 177

1960 LONDON. Hanover Gallery. May–June

1960 PARIS. Galerie Berggruen. June–Sept. (Lithographs. "Série des Phénomènes")

1960 NEW YORK. Peter Deitsch Gallery. Sept. 13–Oct. 7. (Recent lithographs. "Les Phénomènes")

1960 EINDHOVEN. Stedelijk van Abbe Museum. Sept. 24–Oct. 30. (Graphics.) * See bibl. 178. Also shown at the Stedelijk Museum, Amsterdam, Nov. 4–Dec. 12, 1960

1960 PARIS. Galerie Berggruen. Oct.–Nov. (Drawings, in connection with the publication of the book by Daniel Cordier)

1960 NEW YORK. World House Galleries. Oct. 25–Nov. 26.* See bibl. 179

1960 HANOVER. Kestner-Gesellschaft. Oct. 26–Dec. 4.* See bibl. 180

1960 NEW YORK. Cordier & Warren Gallery. Dec. 8, 1960–Jan. 5, 1961. ("One Hundred Drawings of Jean Dubuffet").

1960 PARIS. Musée des Arts Décoratifs. Dec. 16, 1960–Feb. 25, 1961.* See bibl. 181

1961 FRANKFORT. Galerie Daniel Cordier. Mar. 3–Apr. 15. ("Matériologies") *

1962 NEW YORK. Museum of Modern Art. Feb. 19–Apr. 8.* Also exhibited at The Art Institute of Chicago, Los Angeles County Museum of Art

GROUP SHOWS

This list includes only exhibitions for which publications of consequence were issued.

1955 NEW YORK. Museum of Modern Art. May–Aug. 1955. ("The New Decade.") * See bibl. 169. Also exhibited at Minneapolis Institute of Arts, Los Angeles County Museum, San Francisco Museum of Art

1959 NEW YORK. Museum of Modern Art. Sept. 30–Nov. 29. ("New Images of Man.") * See bibl. 174. Also shown at Baltimore Museum of Art

1961 SILKEBORG (Denmark). Silkeborg Museum. ("Dubuffet Grafik.") Graphics of Dubuffet in special exhibition of the collections of the Museum. See bibl. 182

1961 NEW YORK. Museum of Modern Art. Oct. 2–Nov. 12. ("The Art of Assemblage.") * See bibl. 183. Also exhibited at Dallas Museum for Contemporary Arts and San Francisco Museum of Art

Bibliography

Owing to the limited amount of materials actually accessible to the compiler, reliance has been placed on bibliographical lists in authentic sources, frequently by transcription. To a large extent the documentation is based on the extensive and valuable information supplied by Mr. Noël Arnaud in *Cahiers du Collège de Pataphysique*, Dossiers 10/11, 1960 (bibl. 71, 111). Additional comprehensive data are reported in the Musée des Arts Décoratifs catalogue (bibl. 181) and have been used in the form there stated.

Inga Forslund

TEXTS BY DUBUFFET

1 Petit guide du visiteur de l'exposition des lithographies de Jean Dubuffet à la Galerie André. [Paris, The Gallery.] 1945.

> Text also published under the title: "Notice commune" in "Prospectus aux amateurs de tout genre." See bibl. 5.

2 L'Art et le public: [réponse à une enquête]. *Les Lettres Françaises* Année 6 no. 102:3 Apr. 5, 1946.

> Reprinted in *Transition 49* (Paris) no. 5:117–120 1949.

3 L'Auteur répond à quelques objections. *In* Tapié, Michel, Mirobolus, Macadam & Cie. Hautes Pâtes. Paris, Galerie René Drouin, 1946.

> Reprinted in "Prospectus aux amateurs de tout genre." See bibl. 5. Also published under the title: "Réhabilitation de la boue" in *Juin* May 7, 1946 and in *Dialogue* July 1946.

4 Indications descriptives. *In* Tapié, Michel, Mirobolus, Macadam & Cie. Hautes Pâtes. Paris, René Drouin, 1946. See bibl. 89.

5 Prospectus aux amateurs de tout genre. [158] p. Paris, Gallimard, 1946. (Collection "Métamorphoses.")

> Includes "Notice commune."—"L'auteur répond à quelques objections."

6 Causette. *In* "Portraits." Paris, Galerie René Drouin, Oct. 1947.

7 [Preface]. *In* catalogue of "L'exposition Gaston Chaissac." Paris, Galerie Arc-en-Ciel, June 11–July 5, 1947.

8 Lettre à M. Le Directeur des Lettres Françaises au sujet de Charles-Albert Cingria. 1947.

> Mimeographed text in 100 copies.

9 Les Barbus Müller et autres pièces de la statuaire provinciale. *L'Art Brut* (Paris) fasc. 1, ill. 1947.

> Edition of 1,500 copies which, with the exception of 20, were never released.

10 Les Statues de silex de M. Juva. *Les Cahiers de la Pléiade* no. 5: 149-155 Summer 1948.

> Originally published as preface to catalogue of "L'exposition de silex de Juva." Paris, Galerie René Drouin, June 17–July 17, 1948. Mimeographed text in 300 copies. Translated into English: Monsieur Juva's flint statues. *Evergreen Review* v. 4 no. 13:73–78 May–June 1960.

11 "L'Art brut": Miguel Hernandez. *Les Cahiers de la Pléiade* no. 6: 104–108 Fall 1948/Winter 1949.

12 Ler dla canpane par Dubufe J. 1948.

"Texte autographié sur stencil avec gravures sur linoléum, sur bois de caisse . . ." Noted on last page: "L'Art Brut, Noël, 1948." Edition of 165 copies. Reprinted in *Les Cahiers de la Pléiade* no. 7: 141–155 Spring 1949.

13 Lettre à Albert Paraz au sujet de Louis Ferdinand Céline. *Paroles Françaises* Nov. 26, 1948.

14 Joaquim Virens Gironella. *In* catalogue of: "Lièges sculptés de J. V. Gironella." Foyer de l'Art Brut, Nov. 9–Dec. 3, 1948.

Mimeographed text in 300 copies.

15 Anvouaiaje par in nin besil. Paris, The Author, 1949.

"Texte autographié lithographié." 9 original lithographs (6 color).

16 L'Art brut préféré aux arts culturels. Paris, Compagnie de L'Art brut, 1949.

Presentation of exhibition of "L'Art brut" at Galerie René Drouin, Oct. 1949. Edition of 1,000 copies (30 with original linoleum engravings by Miguel Hernandez). See bibl. 166.

17 Réponse à l'enquête de Maurice Lemaître sur le Procès Céline. *Le Libertaire* Jan. 20, 1950.

18 Labonfam abeber par inbo nom. Paris, The Author, 1950.

"Texte autographié lithographié." Edition of 50 copies.

Two pages from bibl. 12

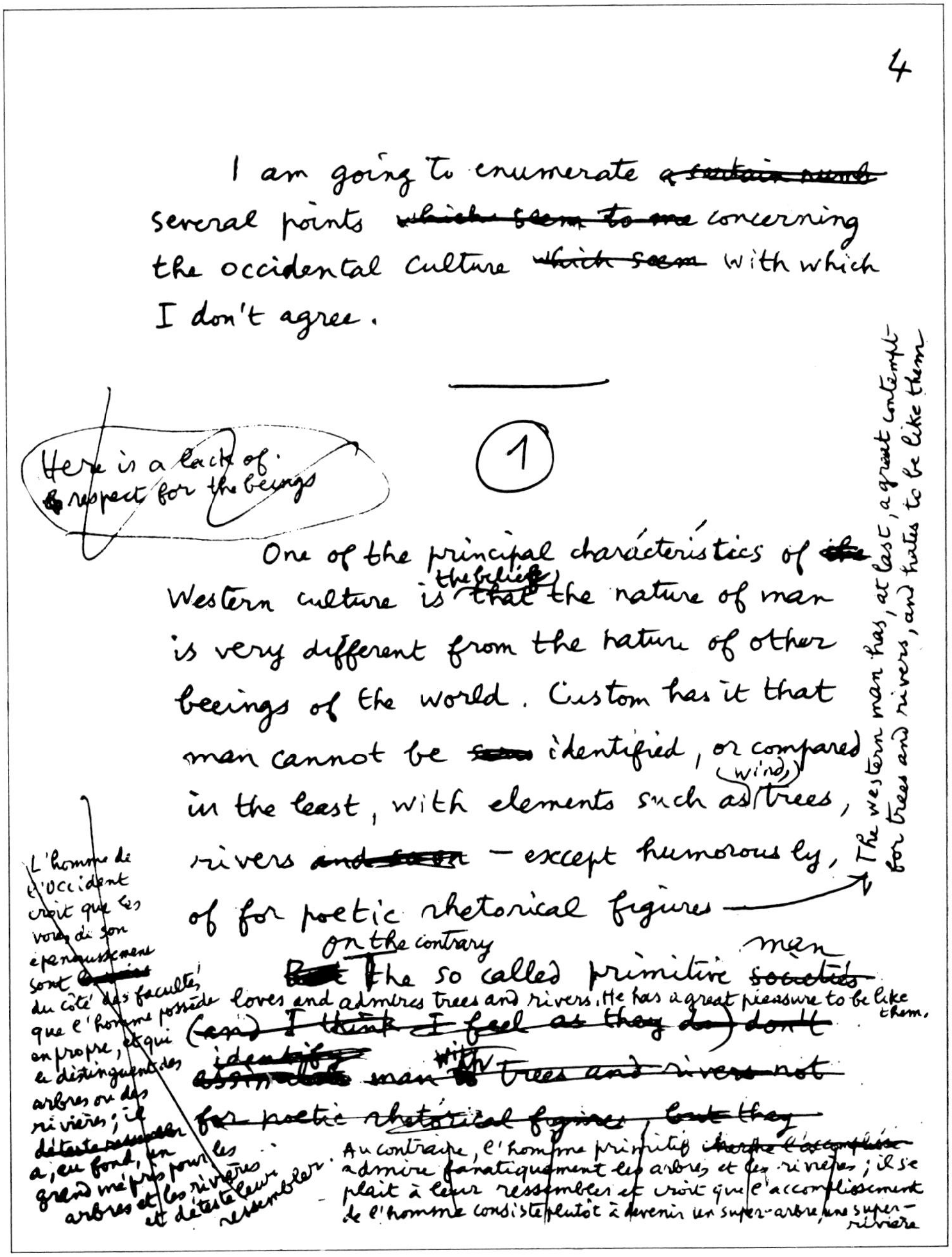

I am going to enumerate a ~~certain numb~~ several points ~~which seem to me~~ concerning the occidental culture ~~which seem~~ with which I don't agree.

———

①

(Here is a lack of. respect for the beings)

One of the principal characteristics of ~~the~~ Western culture is ~~that~~ (the belief) the nature of man is very different from the nature of other beeings of the world. Custom has it that man cannot be ~~seen~~ identified, or compared in the least, with elements such as trees, (wind) rivers ~~and seen~~ — except humorously, of for poetic rhetorical figures —

The western man has, at least, a great contempt for trees and rivers, and hates to be like them

on the contrary

~~But~~ The so called primitive ~~societies~~ men loves and admires trees and rivers. He has a great pleasure to be like them. ~~(and I think I feel as they do) don't~~ ~~identify~~ ~~assimilate man with trees and rivers not~~ ~~for poetic rhetorical figures but they~~

L'homme de l'Occident croit que les voies de son épanouissement sont ~~ou~~ du côté des facultés que l'homme possède en propre, et qui le distinguent des arbres ou des rivières; il a, au fond, un grand mépris pour les arbres et les rivières et déteste leur ressembler

Au contraire, l'homme primitif ~~cherche l'accomplisse~~ admire fanatiquement les arbres et les rivières; il se plaît à leur ressembler et croit que l'accomplissement de l'homme consiste plutôt à devenir un super-arbre, une super-rivière

Page of manuscript for bibl. 25

19 Letter to the editor. *Art News* v. 49 no. 2: 6 Apr. 1950.

20 Lettre à Geert van Bruaene. *Cobra* no. 6 Apr. 1950.

21 Plu kifekler mouinkon nivoua par Dubufe Jan. Saint-Maurice d'Etelan, Edition L'Art du Temps, 1950.
   Edition de luxe of 175 copies. Contains the three previous texts in Dubuffet jargon: Ler dla canpane, Anvouaiaje, Labonfam abeber.

22 Cinq petits inventeurs de la peinture: Paul End, Alcide, Liber, Gasduf, Sylvocq. Lille, Marcel Evrard, 1951.

23 Nomenclature et descriptions des 29 tableaux expédiés à Pierre Matisse à New York. *In* [Dubuffet catalogue]. New York, Pierre Matisse Gallery, Jan. 9–Feb. 3, 1951.

24 Peintures initiatiques d'Alfonso Ossorio. 68 p. Paris, La Pierre Volante, 1951.
   Also numbered edition of 36 copies with an original color lithograph.

25 Anticultural positions. 1951.
   Lecture given at the Arts Club of Chicago, Dec. 1951. Photostatic copy of original manuscript available in the Library of the Museum of Modern Art. Largely reprinted in bibl. 179.

26 [Preface]. *In* [Dubuffet catalogue]. New York, Pierre Matisse Gallery, Feb.–Mar. 1952.
   Original text in French lost. Translated into English by the author in collaboration with Marcel Duchamp.

27 [Preface]. *In* Chaissac, Gaston, Histoires d'un vacher. Paris, Editions Le Courier de Poésie, 1952.
   Reprinted in *La Nouvelle Revue Française* Année 1 no. 11: 929–931 Nov. 1, 1953.

28 Lettre au *Figaro Littéraire* Année 8 no. 387: 3 Sept. 19, 1953.

29 Notes du peintre. *In* Limbour, Georges, Tableau bon levain à vous de cuire la pâte. Paris, René Drouin, 1953.
   See bibl. 76.

30 Is the American avant garde over-rated? *Art Digest* v. 28 no. 2: 10 Oct. 15, 1953.
   A reply contributed to a symposium.

31 Terres radieuses. *In* [Dubuffet catalogue]. Paris, Galerie La Hune, Dec. 1953.
   Presentation of 16 ink drawings.

32 Pourquoi ne croyez vous pas en Dieu?: [réponse à une enquête]. *Le Peignoir de Bain* (Alès) IV, 1954.

33 [Statement]. *In* "The New Decade." New York, Museum of Modern Art, May–Aug. 1955.
   See bibl. 169.

34 [Text]. *In* catalogue of "Dewasne, Dubuffet, Matta." Paris, Galerie Daniel Cordier, Dec. 1956.

35 Empreintes. *Les Lettres Nouvelles* no. 48: 507–527 Apr. 1957.
   Extracts of this text in the catalogue "Dubuffet, Michaux, Wols." Paris, Studio Paul Facchetti, May 21–June 21, 1957.

36 [Postface]. *In* "Tableau d'Assemblages." Paris, Galerie Rive Droite, Apr. 30–May 23, 1957.

37 A chacun sa réalité: [réponse à l'enquête de Pierre Volboudt]. *XXe Siècle* Nouv. sér. no. 9: 24–25 ill. June 1957.

38 Mémoire sur le développement de mes travaux depuis 1952. 1957–1959.
   Typescript in 15 copies. Also printed in the catalogue of the Musée des Arts Décoratifs, Paris, 1960. See bibl. 181.

39 Peindre n'est pas teindre. *In* [Dubuffet catalogue]. Milan, Galleria del Naviglio, Jan. 25–Feb. 14, 1958.

Extracts of "Prospectus aux amateurs de tout genre" (from bibl. 5).

40 Extracts from a preface. *In* Jean Dubuffet. London, Arthur Tooth Gallery, Apr. 29–May 23, 1958.

See bibl. 173. Complete text never published.

41 Oukiva trene sebot par Jandu Bufe. Paris, Collège de Pataphysique, Collection Traître Mot, 1958.

With 4 portraits of Dubuffet by Pierre Bettencourt and 5 drawings by Dubuffet. Edition of 589 copies.

42 Lettre à France-Soir. *France-Soir* Nov. 13, 1958.

43 [Statement]. *In* "New Images of Man." New York, Museum of Modern Art, 1959.

See bibl. 174.

44 Texturologies, Topographies. *In* "Célébration du Sol." Paris, Galerie Daniel Cordier, Apr.–June 1959.

First published in *Les Lettres Nouvelles* Année 7 Nouv. sér. no. 8: 8–10 Apr. 22, 1959.

45 Non merci: [réponse à Herbert Read]. *Les Lettres Nouvelles* Année 7 Nouv. sér. no. 8: 33 Apr. 22, 1959.

46 "L'Art brut." *In* [Catalogue.] Vence, Galerie Les Mages, Aug.–Sept. 1959.

Presentation of the exhibition, organized by Alphonse Chave.

47 La fleur de barbe. [Paris, 1960.]

Handwritten text and illustrations by Jean Dubuffet. Limited edition of 500 numbered copies. Reprinted in *Cahiers du Collège de Pataphysique* Nouv. sér. Dossiers 10/11: 5–12 1960.

48 Texturologier och topografier. *Paletten* no. 1: 2–3 ill. 1960.

In Swedish.

49 Carte de voeux de la Galerie Beyeler, Basel. 1960.

Text and lithograph.

50 Apercevoir. *In* [Dubuffet catalogue]. Paris, Musée des Arts Décoratifs, Dec. 16, 1960–Feb. 25, 1961.

See bibl. 181.

51 [Statement]. *Daedalus* v. 89 no. 1: 95–96 Winter 1960.

AS TU CUEILLI
LA FLEUR DE BARBE
SUR LA MI CÔTE
C'EST LE PRINTEMPS ET VOICI
QUE LA BARBE REVERDIT
S'EN TISSE LE FIL UN LUNDI
A LA FIN DE LA SEMAINE
S'EMBARBE TOUT LE PAYS

Page of text from bibl. 47

Two pages from bibl. 61

ILLUSTRATED BOOKS

52 ELUARD, PAUL. Quelques mots rassemblés pour Monsieur Dubuffet. Paris, 1944.
    1 original lithograph. Edition of 100 copies.

53 SEGHERS, PIERRE. L'Homme du Commun ou Jean Dubuffet. Paris, Edition Poésie 44, 1944.
    2 original lithographs (1 on cover). Edition of 161 copies.

54 FRÉNAUD, ANDRÉ. Vache bleue dans une ville. Paris, Seghers, 1944.
    1 original lithograph. Edition of 150 copies.

55 PONGE, FRANCIS. Matière et mémoire, ou les Lithographs à l'école par Francis Ponge et Jean Dubuffet. [14] p. 34 plates Paris, F. Mourlot, 1945.
    Text by Ponge; 34 original lithographs by Dubuffet. Edition of 60 copies.

56 GUILLEVIC. Elégies. Paris, Edition du Point du Jour, 1946.
    1 original color lithograph. Edition of 306 copies.

57 DUBUFFET, JEAN. Ler dla canpane. 1948.
    See bibl. 12.

58 DUBUFFET, JEAN. Anvouaiaje par in nin besil. 1949.
    See bibl. 15.

59 DUBUFFET, JEAN. Labonfam abeber par imbo nom. 1950.
  See bibl. 18.

60 GUILLEVIC. Les Murs. Poèmes. Paris, Editions du Livre, 1950.
  15 original lithographs (1 on cover). Edition of 172 copies.

61 PAULHAN, JEAN. La Métromanie ou les Dessous de la Capitale. Paris, The Author, 1950.
  "Calligraphié et orné d'images" par Dubuffet. Edition of 150 copies.

62 BETTENCOURT, PIERRE. Le Bal des Ardents. Saint-Maurice-d'Etelan, The Author, 1953.
  1 drawing (butterfly in two colors) on cover. Edition of 120 copies, plus 30 copies with 4 additional drawings.

63 CALET, HENRI. Un grand voyage. Paris, Club Français du Livre, 1953.
  "Reliure frappée au fer du portrait d'Henri Calet par Jean Dubuffet."

64 MARTEL, ANDRÉ. La Djingine du Théophelès. Saint-Maurice-d'Etelan, Edition L'Air du Temps, 1954.
  With 13 "Corps de Dames." Edition of 75 copies.

65 SAGE, KAY. Demain Monsieur Silber . . . By Kay Sage [Mme. Yves Tanguy]. [69] p. plus front. Paris, Seghers, 1957.
  With 1 ink drawing. Edition of 500 copies.

66 DUBUFFET, JEAN. Oukiva trene sebot. 1958.
  See bibl. 41.

67 DUBUFFET, JEAN. La fleur de barbe. 1960.
  See bibl. 47.

BOOKS ON DUBUFFET

68 ARLAND, MARCEL. L'Aventure de Jean Dubuffet. *In* his Chronique de la peinture moderne, p. 36–43 Paris, Editions Corrêa, 1949.

69 ARNAUD, NOËL. Dubuffet. Gravures et lithographies. Catalogue général et introduction par Noël Arnaud. 255 p. incl. Silkeborg 1961.
  Published in connection with a special exhibition of the collections of Silkeborg Museum, 1961.

70 CHARPIER, J. & SEGHERS, PIERRE. L'Art de la peinture. p. 707–709 Paris, Seghers, 1957.

71 COLLÈGE DE PATAPHYSIQUE. Quelques introductions au cosmorama de Jean Dubuffet. N.p. n.d.
  Edition of 299 numbered copies on grand papier rose romanesque, with cover designed by Dubuffet. Also published as *Cahiers du Collège de Pataphysique* Nouv. sér. Dossiers 10/11 1960. See bibl. 111.

72 CORDIER, DANIEL. Les dessins de Jean Dubuffet. Paris, Ditis, 1960.

73 CORDIER, DANIEL. The drawings of Jean Dubuffet. [137] p. incl. 113 ill. New York, Braziller, 1960. Translation of the French edition.

74 FITZSIMMONS, JAMES. Jean Dubuffet: brève introduction à son oeuvre. [72] p. plus 66 plates Brussels, Editions de la Connaissance, 1958.
  Originally published in English in *Quadrum* no. 4: 27–50 ill. 1957.

75 HAFTMANN, WERNER. Painting in the twentieth century. v. 1, p. 332, 360–362, 386.—v. 2, p. 462, 463 New York, Praeger, 1960.

76 Limbour, Georges. Tableau bon levain à vous de cuire la pâte. L'Art brut de Jean Dubuffet. 103 p. incl. 89 ill. (8 col.). New York, Pierre Matisse, 1953.

Includes: "Notes du peintre" p. 91–97.

77 Parrot, Louis. Jean Dubuffet. 19 p. plus 24 plates Paris, Seghers, 1944.

Issued on occasion of the first exhibition at the Galerie René Drouin.

78 Picon, Gaetan. Panorama des idées contemporaines. p. 458 Paris, Nouvelle Revue Française, 1957.

79 Pieyre de Mandiargues, A. Le Belvédère. Paris, Grasset, 1958.

80 Ponente, Nello. Modern painting. Contemporary trends. Tr. from the Italian by James Emmons. p. 66, 100, 118, 159, 164, 165–167, 168 ill. (col. plates) Skira, 1960.

Jacket from bibl. 76

Cover from bibl. 90

81 RAGON, MICHEL. Le cas Dubuffet. *In* his L'Aventure de l'art abstrait, p. 83–88 Paris, Lafont, 1956.

82 RAGON, MICHEL. Dubuffet. Paris, Georges Fall, 1958.

83 RAGON, MICHEL. Dubuffet. 62 p. incl. 12 col. plates New York, Grove Press, 1959.
    Translation of the French edition.

84 RITCHIE, ANDREW CARNDUFF, ed. The New Decade: 22 European painters and sculptors. p. 17–21 incl. ill. New York, Museum of Modern Art, 1955.
    See bibl. 169.

85 SEGHERS, PIERRE. L'Homme du Commun ou Jean Dubuffet. Paris, Edition Poésie 44, 1944.
    2 original lithographs (1 on cover). Edition of 161 copies.

86 SEITZ, WILLIAM. The Art of Assemblage. p. 84, 93–95, 150 New York, Museum of Modern Art, 1961.
    See bibl. 183.

87 SELZ, PETER. New Images of Man. p. 60–67 ill. New York, Museum of Modern Art, 1959.
    See bibl. 174.

88 TAPIÉ, MICHEL. Un art autre où il s'agit de nouveaux dévidages de réel. Paris, Gabriel Giraud, 1952.

89 TAPIÉ, MICHEL. Mirobolus, Macadam & Cie. Hautes Pâtes de Jean Dubuffet. 55 p. incl. ill. Paris, Galerie René Drouin, 1946.
    Reproductions of 32 of the works exhibited at the Galerie René Drouin. Includes: "Indications descriptives" by Dubuffet.

90 VOLBOUDT, PIERRE. Les assemblages de Jean Dubuffet: Signes, sols, sorts. 117 p. ill. 17 plates (9 col.) Paris, XXe Siècle[&] F. Hazan, 1958.
    Issued loose in boxed folio.

ARTICLES ON DUBUFFET

91 ALLOWAY, LAWRENCE. Dubuffet as pastoral. *In* [Dubuffet catalogue.] London, Arthur Tooth Gallery, May 31–June 18, 1960.
    See bibl. 177.

92 ALLOWAY, LAWRENCE. The facts of the matter and the figures involved. *Art News and Review* v. 7 no. 6: 2 April 16, 1955.
    On the exhibition at the Institute of Contemporary Arts, London.

93 ALLOWAY, LAWRENCE. Paris in the 1940s. *Art News and Review* v. 9 no. 21: 1–2 incl. ill. Nov. 9, 1957.

94 ARCANGELI, FRANCESCO. Una situazione non improbabile. *Paragone* (Florence) no. 85: 3–45 January 1957.

95 ARLAND, MARCEL. Jean Dubuffet. *Le Spectateur des Arts* cahier 1: 23–29 ill. Dec. 1944.

96 ARNAUD, NOËL. Chronologie pathologique des expositions de Jean Dubuffet.—Bibliographie & textuaire de Jean Dubuffet. *Cahiers du Collège de Pataphysique* Nouv. sér. Dossiers 10/11: 97–154 1960.
    See also bibl. 71, 111.

97 L'art opérant. *Dossiers acénonètes du Collège de Pataphysique* no. 4 July 14, 1958.

98 ASHTON, DORE. Le peintre malgré lui. *Arts and Architecture* v. 77 no. 1: 7, 30 ill. Jan. 1960.

99 BARILLI, RENATO. La pittura di Dubuffet. *Il Verri* (Milan) Oct. 1959.

100 BERGER, JOHN. The art of unlived life. *New Statesman* v. 55 no. 1417: 601 May 10, 1958.

101 BERGER, JOHN. The arts and entertainment: mud

and others. *New Statesman and Nation* v. 49 no. 1259: 574–575 Apr. 23, 1955.

102 BERTELÉ, RENÉ. Empreintes assemblées de Dubuffet. *XXe Siècle* Nouv. sér. no. 6: 51–52 incl. ill. Jan. 1956.

103 BOERS, F. De snob interesseert zich voor kunst. *Kroniek van Kunst en Kultur* Jahrg. 9 no. 2: 63–64 Feb. 1948.

104 BUTCHER, G. M. Jean Dubuffet. *Arts News and Review* v. 12 no. 9 incl. ill. May 1960.

105 CANADAY, JOHN. Art. Dubuffet display. *New York Times* Nov. 11, 1959.

106 CANADAY, JOHN. Dubuffet and Picasso. *New York Times* Nov. 15, 1959.

107 CHAISSAC, GASTON. A propos de la Métromanie illustrée par J. D. *Voies Nouvelles (Périgueux)* Mar. 24, 1951.

108 CHOAY, FRANÇOISE. Les découvertes d'une rétrospective et la mythologie de la terre dans l'oeuvre de Jean Dubuffet. *Art International* v. 5 no. 1: 20–29 incl. ill. Feb. 1, 1961.

109 CHOAY, FRANÇOISE. Dubuffet et les fascinations de la terre. *France Observateur* May 28, 1960.

110 COURTADES, JACQUES. Jean Dubuffet. *Palaestra* (Amsterdam) Jahrg. 2 no. 4: 90–92 ill. 1948.

110a DELMAS, GLADYS. French art during the occupation. *Magazine of Art* v. 38 no. 3: 88 March 1945.

111 [DUBUFFET dossier.] *Cahiers du Collège de Pataphysique* Nouv. sér. Dossiers 10/11 1960.
The whole issue dedicated to Jean Dubuffet, under title: "Quelques introductions au Cosmorama de Jean Dubuffet, satrape." Includes text by Dubuffet, chronology and documentation by Noël Arnaud. On title page: Viridis Candela. Dossiers acénonètes du Collège de Pataphysique. 10–11.

112 ESCHAPASSE, MAURICE. Dubuffet ou L'Art brut. *Revue de la Pensée Française* Année 13 no. 2: 47–49 Feb. 1954.

113 FITZSIMMONS, JAMES. Dubuffet. *Arts and Architecture* v. 71 no. 5: 8–9 May 1954.

114 FITZSIMMONS, JAMES. Jean Dubuffet. *In* [Dubuffet catalogue.] Leverkusen, 1957.
Biographical note in English. See bibl. 171.

115 FITZSIMMONS, JAMES. Jean Dubuffet: a short introduction to his work. *Quadrum* no. 4: 27–50 incl. ill. col. plates 1957.
Also published in French as a separate with additional illustrations. See bibl. 74.

116 GALLEGO, JULIAN. Jean Dubuffet y el Arte en Bruto. *Goya* no. 19: 32–34 ill. July–Aug. 1957.

117 GENAUER, EMILY. This week in art. *New York World Telegram* Jan. 11, 1947.

118 GERMOZ, ALAIN, Jean Dubuffet, le barbare. *Artes* (Antwerp) no. 8: 25 Apr. 1947.

119 GINDERTAEL, R. V. Jean Dubuffet. *Cimaise* Sér. 1 no. 6: 10 ill. May 1954.

120 GOLDWATER, ROBERT. Dubuffet's diablerie. *View* v. 7 no. 3: 47, 49 Mar. 1947.

121 GOOSSEN, E. C. The texturology of Jean Dubuffet. *Art International* v. 4 no. 8: 31–35 incl. ill (5 col.) Oct. 1960.

122 GREENBERG, CLEMENT. Jean Dubuffet. *The Nation* v. 164 no. 5: 136–137, 139 Feb. 1, 1947.

123 GREENBERG, CLEMENT. Jean Dubuffet et "art brut". *Partisan Review* v. 16 no. 3: 295–297 Mar. 1949.

124 GROHMANN, WILL. Jean Dubuffet. *In* "Lob der Erde." Frankfort, Galerie Daniel Cordier, Dec. 1958–Jan. 1959.

125 GUEGUEN, PIERRE. J. Dubuffet et le rachat de la matière. *Aujourd'hui* no. 20:30–33 ill. Nov.–Dec. 1958.

126 HESS, THOMAS B. Dubuffet paints a picture. *Art News* v. 51 no. 3:30–33 ill. May 1952.

127 HUYGHE, RENÉ. Dubuffet. *Arts* (Paris) no. 68: 1–2 May 17, 1946.

128 JOHNSON, CHARLOTTE BUEL. Two contemporary French abstract expressionists. *Albright Art Gallery: Gallery Notes* v. 21 no. 2:10–18 incl. ill. Summer 1958.

129 LALOUX, FRANÇOIS. L'exposition Jean Dubuffet (Cercle Volney). *Cahiers du Collège de Pataphysique* no. 15 March 14, 1954.

130 LIMBOUR, GEORGES. Au lieu de bottes de sept lieues-, ces jardins. *In* [Dubuffet catalogue.] Paris, Galerie Rive Droite, Apr.–May 1957.

131 LIMBOUR, GEORGES. Célébration du sol. *Les Lettres Nouvelles* Année 7 Nouv. sér. no. 10:30–32 May 6, 1959.

132 LIMBOUR, GEORGES. Description d'un tableau. *Botteghe Oscure* (Rome) 19:28–55 1957.

133 LIMBOUR, GEORGES. Het grafisch werk van Jean Dubuffet. *Museum Journal* (Otterlo) Sér. 6 no. 3:56–61 ill. Sept. 1960.
   Text of the introduction to the catalogue of the exhibition at Eindhoven and Amsterdam, 1960. See bibl. 178.

134 LIMBOUR, GEORGES. Jean Dubuffet. *L'Oeil* no. 25: 36–41 ill. (1 col.) port. Jan. 1957.

135 LIMBOUR, GEORGES. Jean Dubuffet. *In* [Dubuffet catalogue.] London, Institute of Contemporary Arts, Mar. 29–Apr. 30. 1955.
   See bibl. 168. Additional texts by Limbour have appeared in the catalogues of the following exhibitions: Leverkusen. Städtisches Museum Schloss Morsbroich. Aug. 23–Oct. 13, 1957.—Arthur Tooth Gallery, London, Apr. 29–May 23, 1958.—Pierre Matisse Gallery, New York, Nov. 10–Dec. 12, 1959. See bibl. 171, 173, 175.

136 LIMBOUR, GEORGES. Der Maler Jean Dubuffet. *Das Kunstwerk* 11 no. 12:14–21 ill. col. plate June 1958.

137 LIMBOUR, GEORGES. L'Oeuvre récente de Dubuffet: les lithographies. *XXe Siècle* Nouv. sér. Année 22 no. 14:13–16 June 1960.

138 LIMBOUR, GEORGES. Pierres d'exercise philosophique. *Les Temps Modernes* Année 8 no. 91: 1991–2001 June 1953.

139 LIMBOUR, GEORGES. Les Texturologies de Jean Dubuffet. *Art International* v. 2 no. 9/10: 32, 76, 112 ill. Dec. 1958–Jan. 1959.

140 MICHELSON, ANNETTE. Established scandal. *New York Herald Tribune* (Paris) Apr. 29, 1959.

141 PAULHAN, JEAN. Lettre à Jean Dubuffet. *Poésie* 44 Année 5 no. 20: 23–28 2 plates July–Oct. 1944.
   Reprinted in foreword to the catalogue of the exhibition at the Galerie René Drouin, Oct.–Nov. 1944.

142 PAULHAN, JEAN. Letter to Jean Dubuffet. *View* v. 6 no. 2/3: 27, 29 Mar.–Apr. 1946.

143 PIEYRE DE MANDIARGUES, ANDRÉ. Des barbes et des feuilles. *XXe Siècle* Nouv. sér. Année 22 no. 14: 3–12 ill. col. plates June 1960.

144 PIEYRE DE MANDIARGUES, ANDRÉ. Jean Dubuffet ou le point extrême. *Cahiers du Musée de Poche* no. 2:52–61 ill. port. June 1959.

145 RAGON, MICHEL. Jean Dubuffet. *Cimaise* Sér. 5 no. 3:11–22 ill. Jan.–Feb. 1958.
    Includes a report of a conversation with Dubuffet. English translation p. 7–9. Translated into Spanish in *Plastica* (Bogota) no. 11:1–3 ill. Apr.–June 1958.

146 RAIMONDI, GIUSEPPE. L'arte: il "lavoro" di Jean Dubuffet. *Comunità* (Milan) Anno 13 no. 67:70–77 ill. Feb. 1959.
    Reprinted in English and French in *Art International* v. 3 no. 5/6:22–30 ill. 1959.

147 RAIMONDI, GIUSEPPE. Sotto la Villa Aldini. *Il resto del Carlino* (Bologna) Aug. 31, 1958.

148 RAIMONDI, GIUSEPPE. Jean Dubuffet, "pratico della natura." *La Biennale di Venezia* no. 38:18–24 ill. (1 col.) Jan.–Mar. 1960.
    With English summaries.

149 RAUFAST, RÉGINE. Dubuffet ou l'Art primitif vivant. *Formes et Couleurs* Année 6 no. 6 [6] p. ill. 1944.

150 RESTANY, PIERRE. Dubuffet au naturel. *Art International* v. 3 no. 5/6:31–32 ill. 1959.

151 RIBEMONT-DESSAIGNE, GEORGES. Jean Dubuffet à la limite de l'humour. *XXe Siècle* Nouv. sér. no. 8:49–54 ill. (2 col. plates) Jan. 1957.

152 ROUVE, PIERRE. Dubuffet and tradition. *Art News and Review* v. 10 no. 8:3, 11 May 10, 1958.

153 SAGET, JUSTIN. Du beau du bon Dubuffet. Par Justin Saget (Maurice Saillet). *Combat* Nov. 8, 1946.

154 SCHMALENBACH, WERNER. Jean Dubuffet. *In* [Dubuffet catalogue.] Hanover, Kestner-Gesellschaft, Oct. 26–Dec. 4, 1960.
    See bibl. 180.

155 SELZ, PETER. Nouvelles images de l'homme. *L'Oeil* no. 62:46–53 ill. Feb. 1960.
    Extracts of the introduction to "New Images of Man" (from bibl. 174).

156 SIBERT, CLAUDE-HÉLÈNE. Jean Dubuffet et ses créatures. *Cimaise* Sér. 2 no. 2:16 ill. Nov.–Dec. 1954.

157 TALMAY, ALLENE. Controversial painter: Jean Dubuffet. *Vogue* (New York) p. 134–135, 154 ill. May 1, 1952.

158 TAPIÉ, MICHEL. Dubuffet, the terrible. 1–2. *News Post* (Paris) Nov. 1950; Dec. 1950.

159 TWAITES, JOHN ANTHONY. Jean Dubuffet. *Arts Yearbook* 3:130–135 ill. 1959.

160 VIALATTE, ALEXANDRE. Chronique de la vache étonnée. *La Montagne* (Clermond-Ferraud) May 19, 1959.

161 VIALATTE, ALEXANDRE. Chronique des jours d'avril: Dubuffet en Provence. (Joie de l'eskimo. Moeurs de Jean Dubuffet. Moeurs de la chèvre et du vison . . .). *La Montagne* (Clermont-Ferraud) Apr. 14, 1959.

162 VIALATTE, ALEXANDRE. Jean Dubuffet. *In* [Dubuffet catalogue.] Paris, Galerie Rive Gauche, Oct. 19–Nov. 10, 1954.

163 VOLBOUDT, PIERRE. Jean Dubuffet ou les Métamorphoses de l'élémentaire. *XXe Siècle* no. 11:27–31 ill. col. plates 1958.

164 WALRAVENS, JAN. Jean Dubuffet. *Bulletin des Musées Royaux des Beaux-Arts* (Brussels) 4 no. 4:253–258 ill. Dec. 1955.
    Text in Flemish with summary in French.

165 DROUIN, RENÉ, GALERIE. Portraits à ressemblance extraite, à ressemblance cuite et confite dans la mémoire, à ressemblance éclatée dans la mémoire de M. Jean Dubuffet, peintre. [47] p. incl. 20 ill. Paris, 1947.

At head of title: "Les gens sont bien plus beaux qu'ils croient, vive leur vraie figure à la Galerie René Drouin." Exhibition Oct. 7–31, 1947. 78 works. Includes text by J. Dubuffet: Causette.

166 COMPAGNIE DE L'ART BRUT. L'art brut préféré aux arts culturels. [52] p. ill. Paris, 1949.

Exhibition organized by the Compagnie de L'Art Brut, shown at the Galerie René Drouin, Oct. 1949. Text by Dubuffet.

167 CERCLE VOLNEY. Exposition de peintures, dessins et divers travaux exécutés de 1942 à 1954 par Jean Dubuffet. [16] p. incl. 4 ill. Paris, René Drouin, 1954.

Exhibition Mar. 17–Apr. 17, 1954. 193 works.

168 INSTITUTE OF CONTEMPORARY ARTS. Jean Dubuffet. [12] p. 4 ill. London, 1955.

Exhibition Mar. 29–Apr. 30, 1955. 56 works. Preface by Georges Limbour.

169 NEW YORK. MUSEUM OF MODERN ART. The New Decade: 22 European painters and sculptors. Edited by Andrew Carnduff Ritchie. With statements by the artists. 111 p. incl. ill. New York, 1955.

Exhibition May–Aug. 1955. 5 works by Dubuffet. Catalogue p. 107–109. Selected bibliography p. 110–111. Also exhibited at Minneapolis Institute of Arts, Los Angeles County Museum, San Francisco Museum of Art.

170 MATISSE, PIERRE, GALLERY. Exhibition of paintings and "assemblages d'empreintes" executed in 1954–1955 by Jean Dubuffet. [16] p. incl. 14 ill. New York, 1956.

Exhibition Feb. 21–Mar. 17, 1956. 26 works.

171 LEVERKUSEN. STÄDTISCHES MUSEUM. SCHLOSS MORSBROICH. Jean Dubuffet (1943–1957). [11] p. 16 ill. Leverkusen, 1957.

Retrospective exhibition Aug. 23–Oct. 13, 1957. 87 works. Texts by James Fitzsimmons and Georges Limbour.

172 MATISSE, PIERRE, GALLERY. Exhibition of "peintures d'assemblages, graffiti, sols, texturologie" and other recent works done in 1956 and 1957 by Jean Dubuffet. [20] p. incl. 16 ill. New York, 1958.

Exhibition Feb. 4–22, 1958. 20 works.

173 TOOTH, ARTHUR, GALLERY. Jean Dubuffet (1943–1957). 31 ill. London, 1958.

Exhibition Apr. 29–May 23, 1958. 31 works (all reproduced in the catalogue). Texts by Jean Dubuffet and Georges Limbour.

174 NEW YORK. MUSEUM OF MODERN ART. New Images of Man. By Peter Selz. With statements by the artists. 159 p. incl. 110 ill. (11 col.) New York, 1959.

Exhibition Sept. 30–Nov. 29, 1959. 7 works by Dubuffet. Catalogue p. 152–154. Preface by Paul Tillich. Bibliography p. 155–159. Also exhibited at the Baltimore Museum of Art.

175 MATISSE, PIERRE, GALLERY. Jean Dubuffet, retrospective exhibition 1943–1959. [62] p. incl. 76 ill. New York, 1959.

Exhibition Nov. 10–Dec. 12, 1959. 77 works. Text by Georges Limbour.

176 CORDIER, DANIEL, GALERIE. As-tu cueilli la fleur de barbe? [10] p. incl. 11 ill. Paris, 1960.

Exhibition Apr. 27–May 31, 1960. 54 works.

177 TOOTH, ARTHUR, GALLERY. Jean Dubuffet. Eléments botaniques. [34] p. incl. 40 ill. London, 1960.

Exhibition May 31–June 18, 1960. 40 works. Foreword "Dubuffet as pastoral" by Lawrence Alloway.

178 EINDHOVEN. STEDELIJK VAN ABBE MUSEUM. Jean Dubuffet. Grafiek. [44] p. incl. 17 ill. Eindhoven, 1960.

Exhibition Sept. 24–Oct. 30, 1960. Introduction by Georges Limbour (in Dutch). Includes bibliography, short biography and list of exhibitions. Also shown at the Stedelijk Museum, Amsterdam, Nov. 4–Dec. 12, 1960.

179 WORLD HOUSE GALLERIES. J. Dubuffet. [10] p. plus 26 plates (pt. col.) New York, 1960.

Exhibition Oct. 25–Nov. 26, 1960. 40 works. Contains "Anticultural positions," lecture given by Jean Dubuffet in Dec. 1951 at the Arts Club of Chicago.

180 HANOVER. KESTNER-GESELLSCHAFT. Jean Dubuffet. 47 p. incl. ill. Hanover, 1960.

Exhibition Oct. 26–Dec. 4, 1960. 88 works. Organized by Kestner Gesellschaft and Kunsthaus, Zürich. Introduction by Werner Schmalenbach. Includes list of the artist's different periods (p. 21–22). Text in German.

181 PARIS. MUSÉE DES ARTS DÉCORATIFS. Jean Dubuffet. 1942–1960. 398 p. incl. 193 ill. (pt. col.) Paris, 1960.

Retrospective exhibition Dec. 16, 1960–Feb. 25, 1961. 402 works. Catalogue p. 202–398. Contains biography and bibliography (p. 53–98) and texts by Dubuffet: "Apercevoir" (p. 25–27) and "Mémoire sur le développement de mes travaux à partir de 1952" (p. 129–199).

182 SILKEBORG. MUSEUM. Jean Dubuffet. Gravures et lithographies. Catalogue général et introduction par Noël Arnaud. 255 p. incl. ill. Silkeborg (Denmark), 1961.

Complete catalogue of Dubuffet's graphic works, published on the occasion of "Exposition particulière des collections du Musée de Silkeborg." 1961. Same as bibl. 69.

183 NEW YORK. MUSEUM OF MODERN ART. The Art of Assemblage. By William C. Seitz. 176 p. incl. 146 ill. (11 col.) New York, 1961.

Exhibition Oct. 2–Nov. 12, 1961. 7 works by Dubuffet. Catalogue p. 153–165. Bibliography p. 166–173. Also circulated to Dallas Museum for Contemporary Arts and San Francisco Museum of Art.

Index to Illustrations

Accouchement, see *Childbirth*
Ame du Morvan, 90
Arab on a Camel, 38
Arab and Palm Tree, 36
Arab and Palm Trees, 36
Arbre de fluides, see *Tree of Fluids*
Artful Hubbub, 115
Assemblage d'Empreintes, see *Walking in the Bushes; Lady with a Parasol; Obscure Stage at the Foot of a Wall*
Astravagale, 119
Attentive One, 145
Automobile, Flower of Industry, 162
Aveugle, see *Blind One*

Barbe de retours incertains, see *Beard of Uncertain Returns*
Barbes, see *Beard Map; Beard Offering; Beard of Uncertain Returns; Beard Vase*
Bare Table, 130
Bearded Head, 154
Beard Map, 148
Beard Offering, 150
Beard of Uncertain Returns, 147
Beard Vase, 151
Black Eye, 146
Blind One, 156
Blissful Countryside, 13
Blotting Out Memories, 127
Bowery Bum, 60
Book illustrations, 172, 173, 175, 176, 178
Business Prospers, 161
Busy Life, 82
Butterfly Man, 84

Cafetière, see *Coffee Grinder*
Carte de barbe, see *Beard Map*
Chapeau de fourrure, see *Fur Hat*
Charettes, see *My Cart, My Garden*
Chef en tenue de parade, see *Leader in a Parade Uniform*
Chevalier assailli, see *Knight Attacked*
Chevaliers, see *Knight Attacked*

Childbirth, 15
Ciels, see *Ecstasy in the Sky*
Coffee Grinder, 27
Commerce prospère, see *Business Prospers*
Compagne heureuse, see *Blissful Countryside*
Coq à l'oeil, see *Black Eye*
Corps de Dame (Bareiss), 51
Corps de Dame (D. B. C.), 51
Corps de Dames, see *Corps de Dame (Bareiss); Corps de Dame (D. B. C.); Gaudy Bunch of Flowers; Metafisyx; Olympia; Rose Incarnate; Tree of Fluids*
Cow with Fine Teats, 101
Cow with Red Eyes, 100
Cow with the Subtile Nose, 99
Cursed Gossip, 89

Dame à l'ombrelle, see *Lady with a Parasol*
Dentist, 34
Dépenaillé, see *Ragged One*
Desert Track, 44
Désistement, see *Withdrawal*
Door with Couch-Grass, 133

Ecstasy in the Sky, 61
Effacement de souvenirs, see *Blotting Out Memories*
Eléments Botaniques, see *Forest; Sea of Skin; Gardener*
Example Set by the Soil, 141
Extase au ciel, see *Ecstasy in the Sky*
Extravagant One, 94

Fautrier araignée au front, see *Fautrier with Wrinkled Brow*
Fautrier with Wrinkled Brow, 32
Fête de nuit, see *Night Frolic*
Figure-Augure, see *Soothsayer*
Figures-Augures, see *Attentive One; Heights of Marriage; Sententious One; Soothsayer*

Finot tintamarre, see *Artful Hubbub*
Il Flute sur la bosse, see *Fluting on the Hump*
Fluting on the Hump, 39
Forest, 152
Fumeur au mur, see *Smoker by a Wall*
Fur Hat, 93

Garden of Bibi Trompette, 111
Gardener, 153
Gardens of the Highway, 117
Gaudy Bunch of Flowers (Corps de Dame), 50
Geologist, 54
Gerbe Bariolée, see *Gaudy Bunch of Flowers*
Gitane, see *Gypsy*
Grand nu charbonneux, 18
Grand Jazz Band (New Orleans), 23
Grand portrait myth, see *Jules Supervielle, Large Banner Portrait*
Grise Mine, see *Scornful One*
Gypsy, 95

Hautes Pâtes, see *Mirobolus, Macadam & Cie*
Hauts lieux du mariage, see *Heights of Marriage (Portraits of Werner and Nora Schenk)*
Heights of Marriage (Portraits of Werner and Nora Schenk), 143
Histoire naturelle, see *Natural History*
Homme devant un mur, see *Man in Front of a Wall*
Homme au pardessus, see *Man with Raincoat*

I Live in a Happy Country, 118

Jardinier, see *Gardener*
Jardins de la chaussée, see *Gardens of the Highway*
Jazz, see *Grand Jazz Band*
J'habite un riant pays, see *I Live in a Happy Country*

Joë Bousquet in Bed, 33
Joker, 89
Jules Supervielle, Grand Portrait bannière, see Jules Supervielle, Large Banner Portrait
Jules Supervielle, Large Banner Portrait, 35

Knight Attacked, 56

Lady with a Parasol, 104
Landscape with Drunkards, 40
Landscape in Metamorphosis, 69
Landscape with a Partridge, 68
Landscape with Two Personages, 60
Langage du sol, see Voice of the Soil
Layer of Debris at the Foot of a Wall, 122
Leader in a Parade Uniform, 26
Liaisons et raisons, 75
Lieux Cursifs, see Blotting Out Memories
Lieux Momentanés, see Woman with Red Hat Taking a Walk
Life without Man III, 159
Lili in Metallic Black, 29
Lili noir métallique, see Lili in Metallic Black
Limbour, Chicken Droppings, 28
Limbour, façon fiente de poulet, see Limbour, Chicken Droppings
Lit de débris au pied du mur, see Layer of Debris at the Foot of a Wall

Maestro, 89
Magician, 91
Man in the Country, 45
Man in Field, 85
Man in Front of a Wall, 20
Man with Raincoat, 85
Man with a Rose, 41
Marche à pied, see The Walk
Materiologies, see Life without Man III
Maudite commère see Cursed Gossip
Medieval Garden, 111
Mer de peau, see Sea of Skin
Merci beaucoup ma santé toujours excellente..., 20
Messages, see Merci beaucoup my santé toujours excellente...

Metafisyx (Corps de Dame), 49
Métro, 16
Minerva, 24
Mirandoliana, 134
Mirobolus, Macadam & Cie, see Coffee Grinder; Leader in a Parade; Minerva; Touring Club
Mon char, mon jardin, see My Cart, My Garden
Mouleuse de café, see Coffee Grinder
My Cart, My Garden, 108

Natural History, 65
Night Frolic, 57

Oberon, 157
Obscure Stage at the Foot of a Wall, 124
Obscur théâtre au pied du mur, see Obscure Stage at the Foot of a Wall
Offrande de barbe, see Beard Offering
Old Man of the Beach, 155
Olympia (Corps de Dame), 46

Papier mâché masks, 11
Papillons (1953), see Butterfly Man
Papillons (1955), see Garden of Bibi Trompette; Medieval Garden
Partie liée au sol, see Person Attached to the Soil
Pâtes Battues, see Busy Life; Still Life with Passport
Paysage au chieur, see Man in Field
Paysage avec deux personnages see Landscape with Two Personages
Paysage avec êtres tenant de se former, see Landscape in Metamorphosis
Paysage aux ivrognes, see Landscape with Drunkards
Paysage à la perdrix, see Landscape with a Partridge
Paysage avec prise en gelée du ciel, see Landscape with Two Personages
Paysages Grotesques, see Desert Track; Landscape with Drunkards; Man in the Country
Peintures Laquées, see Extravagant One; Fur Hat; Gypsy
Person Attached to the Soil, 136

Personnages Fantômatiques, see Black Eye
Personnages Monolithes, see Artful Hubbub
Petites Statues (1959-1960), see Bearded Head; Blind One; Oberon; Old Man of the Beach; Scornful One
Petites Statues de la Vie Précaire, see Ame du Morvan; Cursed Gossip; Joker; Maestro; Magician; Ragged One
Pierres, see Stone of Dordogne
Piste au désert, see Desert Track
Piste saharienne, see Desert Track
Porte au chiendent, see Door with Couch-Grass
Portrait with Developments, 74
Portrait of Mme Arthur Dubuffet, Grandmother of the Artist, 10
Portraits, see Fautrier with Wrinkled Brow; Joë Bousquet in Bed; Lili in Metallic Black; Limbour, Chicken Droppings; Jules Supervielle, Large Banner Portrait
Promenade buissonneuse, see Walking in the Bushes
Promeneuse au chapeau rouge, see Woman with Red Hat Taking a Walk
Prompt Messenger, 86
Prowling Dog, 114

Ragged One, 88
Rocks and Underbrush, 67
Rocs et brousailles, see Rocks and Underbrush
Rose Incarnate (Corps de Dame), 47

Sahara, see Arab on a Camel; Arab and Palm Tree; Arab and Palm Trees; Desert Track; Fluting on the Hump
Scornful One, 155
Sea of Skin, 152
Sententious One, 143
Smoker by a Wall, 21
Sols et Terrains, see Geologist; Landscape in Metamorphosis; Landscape with a Partridge; Night Frolic; Rocks and Underbrush
Sols nus, see Voice of the Soil

Soothsayer, 142
Spotted Cow, 98
Still Life with Passport, 79
Stone of Dordogne, 59

Table aux pièces d'histoire naturelle,
    see Natural History
Table de forme indécise, see Table of
    Undefined Form
Table nue, see Bare Table
Table of Undefined Form, 58
Tableaux d'Assemblages, see Astra-
    vagale; Door with Couch-Grass;
    Gardens of the Highway; I Live in a
    Happy Country; Layer of Debris at
    the Foot of a Wall
Tables, see Bare Table; Natural His-
    tory; Still Life with Passport; Table
    of Undefined Form; Work Table with
    Letter
Terres Radieuses, see Landscape with
    Two Personages, Liaisons et raisons

Tête barbue, see Bearded Head
Texturologies, see Bare Table; Door
    with Couch-Grass; Example Set by
    the Soil; Texturology X: Rose Mar-
    bleized
Texturology X: Rose Marbleized, 140
Topographies, see Person Attached to
    the Soil
Touring Club, 25
Tourist at a Beautiful Place, 107
Touriste au beau site, see Tourist at a
    Beautiful Place
Tree of Fluids (Corps de Dame), 52

Vache la belle tetonnée, see Cow with
    Fine Teats
Vache au nez subtile, see Cow with the
    Subtile Nose
Vache tachetée, see Spotted Cow
Vaches aux yeux rouges, see Cow with
    Red Eyes

Vaches, see Cow with Fine Teats; Cow
    with Red Eyes; Cow with the Subtile
    Nose; Spotted Cow
Vase de barbe, see Beard Vase
Vie affairée, see Busy Life
Voice of the Soil, 135
Vie exemplaire du sol, see Example Set
    by the Soil
Vie sans l'homme, see Life without
    Man III
Vieux de la plage, see Old Man of the
    Beach
View of Paris—The Life of Pleasure, 17
Vue de Paris, see View of Paris—The
    Life of Pleasure

Walk, The, 164
Walking in the Bushes, 105
Withdrawal, 131
Woman on a Bicycle, 12
Woman with Red Hat Taking a Walk, 76
Work Table with Letter, 70

DATE DUE